PRAISE

Pirtle's joy for life is clearly evident here, and it makes readers want to follow her advice.

RED CITY REVIEW

Every time I pick up this book it's a step forward on my path, it gives me the support I need.

AMAZON VERIFIED REVIEW

I recommend this book for anyone who finds they need more hope for a brighter and lighter tomorrow.

AMAZON VERIFIED REVIEW

JACQUELINE PIRTLE

365 Days of Happiness

Because happiness is a piece of cake!

 THE COMPANION JOURNAL WORKBOOK TO 365 DAYS OF HAPPINESS

A step-by-step guide to being happy

COPYRIGHT

Copyright © 2021 Jacqueline Pirtle
www.FreakyHealer.com
All rights reserved. No part of this book may be reproduced or transmitted in any form or by any means, electronic or mechanical, including photocopying, recording, or by any information storage and retrieval system without the written permission of the publisher, except where permitted by law.

ISBN-13: 978-1-7320851-8-3

Published by: Freaky Healer

Editor-in-chief: Zoe Pirtle
All-round Support: Mitch Pirtle

Book cover design by Kingwood Creations kingwoodcreations.com

Author photo courtesy of Lionel Madiou madious.com

I want to let you know that ***365 Days of Happiness*** is a whole system, consisting of the bestseller ***365 Days of Happiness*** and its companion, this profound ***365 Days of Happiness*** journal workbook.

However, I made it so you can receive the benefit of learning how to live happily solely by journaling through this terrific workbook, while also experiencing the full satisfaction by adding reading the daily passages in the book ***365 Days of Happiness***. Either way, I know you'll love my inspirational teachings.

Also, the book ***365 Days of Happiness*** is available as a companion mobile application, for both Android and iPhone. You can find out more at www.freakyhealer.com.

So before you dive in, I want to thank you for hopping on the happiness train with me! I truly hope you enjoy ***365 Days of Happiness*** as much as I loved writing it, and if you do, it would be wonderful if you could take a short minute and leave a review on Amazon.com and Goodreads.com as soon as you can.

Your kind feedback helps other readers find my books easier, and be happy faster. Consider it a happy deed for the world.

Thank you!

ACKNOWLEDGMENTS

Let's be honest here... I have a dream team!

I could not have finished this book without the help of talented, creative, high-for-life, and phenomenal professionals.

From the bottom of my heart, I want to thank Zoe Pirtle for her editorial mastery; Mitch Pirtle for his all-round support; kingwoodcreations.com for their fun and polished book cover design; and madiouART.com for an amazing photo shoot.

I'd also like to extend a huge "Thank You!" to everyone and everything that cheered me on to expand **365 Days of Happiness** into deeper potency through creating this beautiful journal workbook.

It's a fun ride with you all!

Imagine that you are a bee, living your new day, jumping from happiness to happiness. Every jump you take, some happiness sticks on your being; like pollen on the bee. It adds up, resulting in you getting happier and happier.

Now imagine that as this happy bee you also journal about your happy bee-life—making happiness stick better, so much so that other bees are wondering how.

That is what reading 365 Days of Happiness and journaling about the questions in this workbook will do for you.

So what are you waiting for?

Go happy-ing, go buzzing!

DEDICATION

*I dedicate this journal workbook to all **365 Days of Happiness** fans - new and old - and to everyone who's sticking with me and my passion of helping people to live more conscious, mindful, and happier lives.*

You mean the world to the universe!

INTRODUCTION

Dear happiness seeker!

I am absolutely thrilled that you chose to go all in for your happiness quest and are, hopefully, reading the daily passages in my bestseller **365 Days of Happiness** while journaling in this workbook, filled with millions of high-for-life questions, shifting you closer to yourself and reaching daily happiness.

As I mentioned in the book, **365 Days of Happiness**, you might think it's hard or even impossible to be happy every single day but it's not—no matter what is happening you can always change from being unhappy to BE and live your own happiness. By BE, I mean your whole YOU - body, mind, soul, and consciousness - being happy and by live, I mean you experiencing this physical life with all your senses as happy.

It's proven that a happy life is fun and fulfilling, that a happy being has a healthy physical body with a mind capable of producing joyous thoughts, and that a happy heart is easy to connect to while consciousness latches onto this high-for-life way of living—hence, things just go right. Plus you make the world a better place when you are happy because you take

INTRODUCTION

everything and everyone with you on this joy-ride, since all is always connected and ONE.

I truly BELIEVE that our truth in this physical life is to BE and live happily, and KNOW that everyone deserves to learn how to achieve that.

So go, read your daily passage in the book, then come on over and journal your heart out—knowing that happiness is a live moment-to-moment feeling showing up in many different ways. There is never a right or wrong way, no imperfect or perfect joy, and certainly never a good or bad time for happiness. There is only the moment when you start by choosing, committing, and learning how to BE and live happily.

Let's unleash this pure positive energy of your whole being, and get you the deepest understanding of yourself and life—a knowing that's beyond your physical limitations.

This proven and terrific yes-sayer system from the book ***365 Days of Happiness***, together with this journal workbook, supports you in diving happily and vividly into the adventure of your phenomenal life—and to BE and live your happiness.

Happiest,
    Jacqueline Pirtle

Day 1

Amazing things will happen when you start a love affair with your own happiness!

What do these words activate in you? How does a thriving relationship with your happiness look like? What feelings are involved? What activities will you do; dancing, singing, reading, or laughing? Get all wild and word-smart with your happiness.

That IS happiness!

Day 2

Everything and everyone together make up this magnificent ocean of vibrating energy that is our beautiful universe!

When you think about one-ness, what emotions do you sense? Are they feelings of support, love, peace, or even *I can do anything*? What kind of energy are you intending to show up as today? How will you BE and live connected and as ONE with all?

_____
_____
_____
_____
_____
_____
_____
_____
_____
_____
_____
_____
_____
_____
_____
_____
_____

That IS happiness!

Day 3

The best cookie recipe makes delicious and enjoyable cookies! The best happiness recipe makes a delicious and enjoyable life!

What is your best recipe to live your new day in pure bliss? Is it smiling more, eating cleaner food, or finding more quiet time to meditate? Write what measures you will take to guarantee that your time today is beautiful beyond imagination.

_____
_____
_____
_____
_____
_____
_____
_____
_____
_____
_____
_____
_____
_____
_____
_____
_____
_____

That IS happiness!

Day 4

Imagine you are waking up to these exciting words: "Good morning beautiful being! I am happy you opened your eyes today. Get ready and come, because we have someone gorgeous waiting impatiently for you." You ask "Who is it?" It's your new day!

How does that feel for you? Exciting? Magical? List how vividly you will dance with your new day to co-create magic! Write about your loving flow with time!

_____
_____
_____
_____
_____
_____
_____
_____
_____
_____
_____
_____
_____
_____
_____

That IS happiness!

Day 5

Personalize the "when" and the "what" that shifts you to BE and live in your own high-for-life frequency!

Journal away into your land of bliss, and about what it is that gets you smiling and dancing without a care in the world.

That IS happiness!

Day 6

Imagine a bird! Free to fly whenever it wants, and wherever it wants.

What is freedom for you? What does freedom feel like? What freedom are you going to create today—for yourself and for others? Give your words the freedom to be written.

_____
_____
_____
_____
_____
_____
_____
_____
_____
_____
_____
_____
_____
_____
_____
_____
_____
_____

That IS happiness!

Day 7

Imagine a person laughing so hard that tears are rolling down their cheeks.

What does this visualization activate in you? Does it make you feel better, are you cracking a smile too? Plan ahead by writing about all the laughs, smiles, and giggles you will create today! Who will you have such fun with?

_____
_____
_____
_____
_____
_____
_____
_____
_____
_____
_____
_____
_____
_____
_____
_____
_____

That IS happiness!

Day 8

Wish lists are magical, they come with the energy of desires, wishes, hope, happiness, gifts, dreams, and feel-good intentions.

When was the last time you made a self-care wishlist for yourself? Delve into it, writing your intentions with eagerness and joy—and throw some material wishes in there too!

_____
_____
_____
_____
_____
_____
_____
_____
_____
_____
_____
_____
_____
_____
_____
_____
_____
_____
_____
_____

That IS happiness!

Day 9

You matter!!!

That's a good one, isn't it? Why do you think you matter? Write about every little inch of your physical body, your mind, your heart, and your consciousness—and what importance you as a whole being carry. Be bold and self-brag a lot here!

That IS happiness!

Day 10

Imagine you are holding a bug catcher net in your hands, but instead of catching insects, you are catching smiles.

How will you catch and receive millions of smiles in your new day? By smiling often too?

_____
_____
_____
_____
_____
_____
_____
_____
_____
_____
_____
_____
_____
_____
_____
_____
_____
_____
_____
_____

That IS happiness!

Day 11

Imagination is your most personal and powerful happiness creator, because there are no limits.

What is imagination for you? How does it feel; creative, fun, and magical? What is the first happy imagination that pops into your mind? Describe this wonder in depth and length!

That IS happiness!

Day 12

Imagine the most beautiful and magical palace ever!

What does it look like, how does it feel to live in it, and how do you take care of it? Be regal about your answers and write them down. Now think of this palace being your physical body and replace "palace" with "my physical body." Those are some royal insights!

That IS happiness!

Day 13

When you check in with yourself, you gain knowledge, understanding, and wisdom!

No really, you do! How will you check in with yourself? What questions will you ask? And how many times are you going to check in today? Make your plan!

That IS happiness!

Day 14

Imagine you are writing a good old-fashioned love letter.

Go on, write one to yourself, a loved one, your pet, the sky, or the moon. Or even to your favorite chocolate. Just do it! Then enjoy the shift in energy you have accomplished with such a lovely exercise.

_____
_____
_____
_____
_____
_____
_____
_____
_____
_____
_____
_____
_____
_____
_____
_____
_____
_____
_____
_____

That IS happiness!

Day 15

Be clear with how you are, when in your personal high-for-life frequency!

What does it feel like for you when you are over the moon happy? How do you see your life and what are your thoughts when you feel good? Write about being in your high-for-life frequency.

That IS happiness!

Day 16

Imagine waking up, smiling, and saying, "This is already and will be the best day ever!"

What does your *best day ever* look like? How do you want to feel, what are your desires, wishes, and goals for your new day? What food and drinks will you enjoy? Get writing and don't hold back because we are talking about your best day ever after all!

_____
_____
_____
_____
_____
_____
_____
_____
_____
_____
_____
_____
_____
_____
_____
_____
_____

That IS happiness!

Day 17

Are you happy right now?

If yes, write down what makes you happy right now! If no, write down what would make you happy right now—and of course, go do what tickles your joy!

_____

That IS happiness!

Day 18

Imagine your own perfect high-for-life walking path!

What does it look like? What scenery do you love? Nature, city, beach? What season are you thinking of? What energy will it have; playful, loving, peaceful? Imagine yourself walking on it—or sitting if that makes you happier. Then write about it, and stay in this well-feeling frequency all day long.

That IS happiness!

Day 19

Feel, feel, and feel some more!

What feelings would you like to feel more of? How would you like to feel more often? And how can you create your desired emotions? Be very clear here, make a list and an action plan.

_____
_____
_____
_____
_____
_____
_____
_____
_____
_____
_____
_____
_____
_____
_____
_____
_____
_____
_____
_____
_____

That IS happiness!

Day 20

Imagine you do the same things at the same time every single day!

Now imagine you don't! Feel the energy of excitement, adventure, and inspiration this creates. Make your list of things that you are going to do differently today. Choose at least 10, because hey, I know you can do it!

_____
_____
_____
_____
_____
_____
_____
_____
_____
_____
_____
_____
_____
_____
_____
_____
_____
_____
_____
_____

That IS happiness!

Day 23

We live in a universe where everything is made of energy and vibrates in different frequencies.

What is a higher vibing energy for you? Happiness, joy, or bliss? How does it feel? What high vibing energies do you want more—and will allow for yourself? Write your long list of high-for-life energies.

That IS happiness!

Day 24

Miracles are like cakes! Someone's gotta make them!

What miracles do you desire making? What recipe are you going to use? How open are you to allow them? And what is your plan for receiving them? Write your miracle-details!

_____
_____
_____
_____
_____
_____
_____
_____
_____
_____
_____
_____
_____
_____
_____
_____
_____
_____
_____

That IS happiness!

Day 25

Imagine that you are running or speed walking in nature.

How happy are you to speed walk towards your goals today, or would you rather enjoy a slow hike with lots of opportunity for unplanned magic? Both are applaudable ways. Journal about your perfect speed in your new day today!

That IS happiness!

Day 26

Make your energetic space wide, and root deep!

Close your eyes—feel your energetic wideness and deep rootedness. Breathe into this essence, then journal about how amazing this feels for you, being wide and deep.

_____
_____
_____
_____
_____
_____
_____
_____
_____
_____
_____
_____
_____
_____
_____
_____
_____
_____
_____
_____
_____

That IS happiness!

Day 27

Imagine you are waking up, and all you can think of is "I love everything!"

What does that mean for you? How do you feel about loving everything? Feel into your heart space and ask what you could love more or newly. Make your love-list and set those loving intentions.

_____
_____
_____
_____
_____
_____
_____
_____
_____
_____
_____
_____
_____
_____
_____
_____
_____
_____
_____
_____

That IS happiness!

Day 28

Kindness is a necessity for happiness and health!

What is kindness for you? How does it feel like? What kindness can you show to yourself and others today? Write your heart out about kindness!

_____
_____
_____
_____
_____
_____
_____
_____
_____
_____
_____
_____
_____
_____
_____
_____
_____
_____
_____
_____

That IS happiness!

Day 29

Imagine you are looking at a baby, human or animal.

Feel the love and "awww" that you just shifted into. Feel the gentleness and perfection of life and nature in this. Knowing that you are life and also nature, what does that mean for you and your feelings towards yourself? Where could you feel this goodness in your new day over and over?

That IS happiness!

Day 30

Be conscious about all your forward steps you will take in your new day!

A step is movement and forward means ahead! What forward movement can you initiate in your thoughts, feelings, and actions today and what improvements can you focus on? Make your *I am moving forward* list!

_____
_____
_____
_____
_____
_____
_____
_____
_____
_____
_____
_____
_____
_____
_____
_____
_____
_____

That IS happiness!

Day 31

Imagine standing on the top of a mountain with both of your arms stretched high up in the air. You close your eyes, you breathe deep, and think (or say or shout!) "I AM alive!"

How does that feel for you? What does being alive mean for you? How can you show up as *more alive than ever* in your new day? Journal about the power you gain in this being-alive-happening!

_____
_____
_____
_____
_____
_____
_____
_____
_____
_____
_____
_____
_____
_____
_____
_____
_____

That IS happiness!

Day 32

The most powerful and stable place for you to BE and live in is your heart. It's also where the most powerful and stable energy for you to live through is created—your love!

What does your heart and love resemble for you? Strength, power, healing? How does your love feel? Put your phenomenal love-feelings onto paper.

___
___
___
___
___
___
___
___
___
___
___
___
___
___
___
___
___
___

That IS happiness!

Day 33

__Imagine you are the proud owner of a small spa hotel, taking great pride in giving your guests an amazing experience while staying at your magnificent place.__

How does it feel to serve guests luxuriously, and what is pride for you? How can you give yourself a big piece of that same pampering today? Put your self-pampering intentions into words.

That IS happiness!

Day 34

Mindfully present!

What is mindfulness for you? What does *being present mean*? How can you be more mindful and present—combine these two magical ways of being and living? Go on, *write* ahead!

That IS happiness!

Day 35

Imagine a child looking up into the sky, saying "I believe…!"

What can you believe in again, or even newly, the same way that this child is believing? Write your magical believe-list!

_____
_____
_____
_____
_____
_____
_____
_____
_____
_____
_____
_____
_____
_____
_____
_____
_____
_____
_____
_____

That IS happiness!

Day 36

Are you chit-chatting all day long with what is in your awareness?

How can you get over the first awkward bump of being a professional chit-chatter-with-everything in your new day? What will you talk to first, and then after that, squeeze all the information it has out of it? Make your chat case here!

_____
_____
_____
_____
_____
_____
_____
_____
_____
_____
_____
_____
_____
_____
_____
_____
_____

That IS happiness!

Day 37

Imagine someone you love is asking you to do something for them. You get all excited and feel very special, important, trusted, and loved by their request. You go all out, and give your absolute best to do this for them with your purest love. There is a lot of trust, appreciation, respect, gratefulness, happiness, and love created by them asking you!

Where could you jump over your old habits of "asking for help is weak" and instead ask for help—creating all these high-for-life energies for yourself and your helpers?

That IS happiness!

Day 38

Every rejection is a sign that the universe has your back.

What rejection can you shift to being a good thing, a gift, and a supportive way of the universe having your back, because something better is around the corner or it was not the most fitting for you? Get writing!

___

That IS happiness!

Day 39

Imagine sticking a spoon of honey into your mouth. Close your eyes and taste its sweetness.

What sort of sweetness can you be, create, give, and experience in your new day today? Write down your sweet-y-list!

That IS happiness!

Day 40

Feel pleasure!

Oh that should feel pleasurable, to write your own pleasure list! Go on a pleasure-trip!

That IS happiness!

Day 41

Imagine you are waking up to your new day! Your body, mind, soul, and consciousness are all fresh and clean.

How amazing is that! Write about this freshness—how it feels, and how you think, see, smell, taste, and hear about everything and everyone in this fresh state.

That IS happiness!

Day 42

"I wonder..."

How do you feel when you wonder? Perhaps magical? What does wonder mean for you, and what could you possibly wonder about—and drench everything in magic by doing so? What are you waiting for, wonder and write!

That IS happiness!

Day 43

Imagine yourself entering a small crystal and gem store.

How do you feel around all these glimmering and grounding energies? Inspired, alive, and supported? Now imagine that your new day is like that gem store—what sparkles and glamorous moments are you looking forward to or could you create for yourself? Then imagine that you are a gem. How will you live your new day as this preciousness? Write, gem, write!

That IS happiness!

Day 44

A joyful life is created by practicing to be amused by all—because there is nothing ever serious enough to be serious about, but there is always everything amusing enough to be amused by.

This should be fun... What amusement and humor can and will you whip up for today? Write and laugh, then write and laugh some more!

That IS happiness!

Day 45

What or which irritation-angel is in your face? Every un-fitting person or happening (both are irritation-angels) gives you the possibility to think, see, hear, taste, smell, and feel what you are ready to experience.

What or which irritation angel could you openly accept, respect, appreciate, thank, and even love today? Make your angel list and get "thanking!"

_____
_____
_____
_____
_____
_____
_____
_____
_____
_____
_____
_____
_____
_____
_____
_____
_____

That IS happiness!

Day 46

Imagine a colorful, super-sized balloon that you get to fill with all your wishes, dreams, and desires!

Write your wishlist - for yourself, others, and earth - and imagine filling this balloon, letting it fly, and once high up having it pop to shower you and the whole world with your wishes, dreams, and desires.

_____
_____
_____
_____
_____
_____
_____
_____
_____
_____
_____
_____
_____
_____
_____
_____
_____
_____

That IS happiness!

Day 47

The good goose bumps! You know the ones you get when you listen to a beautiful and moving song, or see a breathtaking scenery? Those are the "good goose bumps" that I am talking about.

What feelings are in a good goose bump for you? Excitement, happiness, being in love? What goose bump moments can and will you create for yourself today? Make this list super long!

_____
_____
_____
_____
_____
_____
_____
_____
_____
_____
_____
_____
_____
_____
_____
_____
_____
_____

That IS happiness!

DAY 48

Imagine you are saying "NO" to something or someone that is not fitting or feeling good to you!

What will you say "NO" to today? Who will you say "NO" to? Write your no-list and add, "That's a YES to myself!" at the end of every no-intent—because after all, every "NO" is a "YES" to what is fitting for you.

That IS happiness!

Day 49

Do you ever feel you have to shift yourself into a certain way of being or behaving in order to do something?

Relax, the only shift you need is your shift to BE and live in your heart—because it knows and is always right! How will you align with yourself today? Meditation, conversations with your heart, or through play and laughter? Write about how you will treasure the flow of being you in your new day!

That IS happiness!

Day 50

Just as a simple and basic meal of eggs sunny-side-up and toast (or any other simple meal) can bring so much comfort and happiness, a simple and basic life attitude can bring you comfort, peace, love, light, and happiness too.

Make a list of your basic life attitudes that you can and will enjoy today! Examples are slowing down, breathing consciously, or smiling with no reason.

_____
_____
_____
_____
_____
_____
_____
_____
_____
_____
_____
_____
_____
_____
_____
_____

That IS happiness!

Day 51

Imagine that you have a "Magical Blessing Wand." With that wand, you get to bless everything and everyone you encounter in your new day. Once touched by your blessings, miracles can happen.

Oh my, what will you bless today? We are looking for an endless list here!

That IS happiness!

Day 52

Have an intention-setting "chit-chat" with yourself when you wake up! Ask yourself, "What and how do I want to feel today?" Keep it simple and trust the first word you hear.

Write down your chitter-chatter and be descriptive about your answers. Even better, come up with more questions and enjoy the creative answers you get.

_____
_____
_____
_____
_____
_____
_____
_____
_____
_____
_____
_____
_____
_____
_____
_____
_____

That IS happiness!

Day 53

Imagine you are watching a good drama movie.

How does drama feel for you? Intense, exhausting, or not for you and especially not every day? Write down your rock solid plans to avoid all drama today—to leave drama where it belongs, in a drama film, enjoyed lightly and periodically.

_____
_____
_____
_____
_____
_____
_____
_____
_____
_____
_____
_____
_____
_____
_____
_____
_____
_____
_____
_____

That IS happiness!

Day 54

What do you love right now? Ask yourself this question first thing waking up, once every hour in your new day, and last thing before you fall asleep. Set a love-alarm to remind you!

That's easy and is in no need of explanation—get writing with your "I love..." list! Make it lovingly long.

_____
_____
_____
_____
_____
_____
_____
_____
_____
_____
_____
_____
_____
_____
_____
_____
_____
_____
_____
_____

That IS happiness!

Day 55

Imagine a beautiful and delicious apple! That apple is an apple! It grows like an apple, looks and behaves like an apple, tastes like an apple, and it successfully enchants everyone as an apple. The apple is true to it being an apple, and that is why it successfully can shine bright and tasty, as an apple.

What will you do to stay true to being your unique apple today—versus pretending to be an onion instead?

That IS happiness!

Day 56

Sharing is caring!

List please! What will you share today? The closer to your heart, the bigger the sharing and caring—just saying!

_____
_____
_____
_____
_____
_____
_____
_____
_____
_____
_____
_____
_____
_____
_____
_____
_____
_____
_____
_____

That IS happiness!

Day 57

Imagine a loving parent! They can be human or animal. Visualize how that parent serves their children and family with help, love, kindness, gifts, happiness, compliments, nice words, and care.

What is serving? What does serving feel like to you? How can you serve today? What or who can you serve? Don't forget to list how you will serve yourself too.

That IS happiness!

Day 58

Is there "a good use and need" for it?

What feelings, happenings, or people can you shed today? What can you let go of? List what has no good use for you - what does not feel good to you - and then imagine that what's written down is now out of sight!

_____
_____
_____
_____
_____
_____
_____
_____
_____
_____
_____
_____
_____
_____
_____
_____
_____
_____
_____

That IS happiness!

Day 59

Imagine that you cover all your floors with glitter!

Some might say, "What a mess!" But the reaction I'm hoping for is, "What a sparkling imagination!" Playful and playful-ness is what we are looking for here. What can you sparkle-up in your new day? Your daily routine? People? Your home? What glittery moments can you admire—like water drops, smiling eyes, shiny objects?

That IS happiness!

Day 60

Think of what a BFF does for you... Think what you do for a BFF...

What feelings does this initiate for you? Love, support, always rooting for each other and only wanting the best for each other? How can you shift these beautiful emotions towards your food and nourish yourself with a high quality intake that, in return, is your BFF for life?

That IS happiness!

Day 61

Imagine that you are in an elevator going up!

Upwards is the essence here! What in your life can you lift and feel better about, speak higher of, think more positively about, or create happier? What is your upwards-list?

_____
_____
_____
_____
_____
_____
_____
_____
_____
_____
_____
_____
_____
_____
_____
_____
_____
_____
_____
_____

That IS happiness!

Day 62

Are you not sure anymore? If so, take a timeout! Go inward—breathe and recharge. Remind yourself of the reasons you decided to do what you are doing, when your decision was all new and fresh.

What decisions are you not sure about anymore? List your reasons for deciding that way originally. Do your reasons still fit, or do you need new reasons? Do you need to change your decision altogether?

That IS happiness!

Day 63

Imagine a beautiful wedding!

Let yourself be swooped up by this celebratory event. Then use descriptive words to write about how you will make your new day worthy and special, and the happiest gathering of your life.

That IS happiness!

Day 64

"I am caressed!" Caressed comes with an energy of gentle, loving, sweet, taken care of, and touched.

What does being caressed mean for you? How do you feel when being caressed? What soft words can you use to describe this state of being? How will you create caressed-ness for yourself in your new day?

_____
_____
_____
_____
_____
_____
_____
_____
_____
_____
_____
_____
_____
_____
_____
_____

That IS happiness!

Day 65

Imagine your favorite car! See it and feel how much you admire and love it. Think of all the different parts your favorite car is made of. Some are visible and make the amazing look of that car, while others are not visible and might not be that attractive to look at. But it takes every part to make this favorite car of yours, and you love them all.

Now take that favorite feeling into your whole being and all the different parts that make up you—your body, mind, soul, and consciousness. Write about how you will cherish and admire yourself in your new day.

That IS happiness!

Day 66

"Honor" is your magic for the day!

How does honor, and honoring, look for you? What feelings are attached to the word honor? What and who will you honor today—yourself? How will you do it?

That IS happiness!

Day 67

Imagine a gray and rainy day!

How can you make this gray and rainy day colorful? How can you, despite the darkness, have a blast-filled day? And if you happen to love gray and rainy, what will you do to keep the fun going once the sun comes out? Go on, write colorfully!

_____
_____
_____
_____
_____
_____
_____
_____
_____
_____
_____
_____
_____
_____
_____
_____
_____
_____
_____

That IS happiness!

Day 68

Today is the day!

Let yourself in on what that means for you! What will you do, feel, think, be, and experience in your "the day?"

_____
_____
_____
_____
_____
_____
_____
_____
_____
_____
_____
_____
_____
_____
_____
_____
_____
_____
_____
_____

That IS happiness!

Day 69

Imagine this is what happens when you leave your house in your new day: You walk to your car and spot a heart-shaped leaf. When you drive down the road, you see a heart-shaped sign in a window. When you go to lunch, you notice a heart-shaped chocolate. When you get back to work, you find a coworker with a heart on their shirt. When you leave work, you see a heart-shaped cloud in the sky. And when you get back home, your family gives you a card with a heart on it.

Set a written intention to focus on all hearts - and all feelings that a heart represents for you - in your new day. What will you say to these millions of hearts when they pop up? Will you thank them for the reminder, and tell them, "I love you!"?

_____
_____
_____
_____
_____
_____
_____
_____
_____
_____

That IS happiness!

Day 70

This is a love message from the universe: Dear shining, powerful star, uniquely intelligent and magical being, I want to tell you that...

Write yourself your own and unique love message from the universe! Remember the universe loves you unconditionally, has an infinite amount of beautiful messages for you, and always has your back. Go on, make it count!

That IS happiness!

Day 71

Imagine sitting on the deck of a cottage! Suddenly, a fox runs by. He stops and stares at you. You both have a co-creating moment together. Then, he keeps on running through the land belonging to the cottage. Fox magic happened, just like that! You are in awe, and feel that this fox gifted you with a "Wow!" moment. What an experience!

What surprising and special things could you possibly see, hear, smell, or even taste while co-creating with everything and everyone in your new day? What surprising special things could you open up to receive today?

_____
_____
_____
_____
_____
_____
_____
_____
_____
_____
_____
_____
_____
_____

That IS happiness!

Day 72

Every experience shapes you! Constantly being shaped means you change, move forward, learn more about yourself, and become more and more your unique you. How cool is that?!

What experiences of joy have shaped you most and what blissful ones are you looking forward to? What happenings of lesser fun can you accept, respect, appreciate, thank, and love for lending you a dear hand to develop yourself?

_____
_____
_____
_____
_____
_____
_____
_____
_____
_____
_____
_____
_____
_____
_____

That IS happiness!

Day 73

Don't be sorry for anything or anyone! Being sorry for someone who's experiencing something unpleasant or having a hard time, means you are sorry for them to receive the gift of shaping up, shifting closer to their truth, and moving forward in their journey.

Who can you stop being sorry for, and instead, start celebrating them and their experiences while cheering them on in their own unique life development? Write those beings down, breathe, and let go with a regal smile.

That IS happiness!

Day 74

Imagine you stand on the side of a busy road, and give every person that drives or walks by a flower and a smile.

How does that feel? Exciting, fun, and happy? Who could you bless with joy, instead of un-happiness, today? Yourself? Others? Make your list and set a written intent, for you to walk your path in smiles and bliss!

That IS happiness!

Day 75

Pick an adjective that shifts you to BE and live in your high-for-life frequency!

This does not need a deep explanation—aside from expressing that you should pick more than one and only phenomenal ones! Write your list and about how they make you feel. Use them in your new day—say, think, and feel them often.

That IS happiness!

Day 76

Imagine you encounter a squirrel that is desperately trying to fly like a bird.

Do you do that, trying to be someone else? Journal about how you will stand in your middle of being truly who you are. Be very strong and potent about it!

That IS happiness!

Day 77

Think of all the street and traffic signs! They are always there and everywhere. They give clear directions on what to do and what not to do; where to go and where not to go, and they inform everyone how everything has to be, which creates great clarity.

Do you have your signs up? What kind of clarity that advocates what fits for you are you giving, holding up, voicing, and standing tall and proud with? Go on, make your list of signs and write about how you will keep them up.

That IS happiness!

Day 78

Imagine a robot with no feelings! It simply does what it needs to do, without feeling anything. It gets everything done in a very business-like way. Now imagine this robot can suddenly feel. So everything it does, is now accompanied by a feeling. Being just became very vivid and colorfully fun for that robot. It actually feels alive now.

I want you to be the robot with feelings! How is that for you? What feelings will you allow yourself to feel—new and old ones, low and high ones? List all of them!

_____
_____
_____
_____
_____
_____
_____
_____
_____
_____
_____
_____
_____
_____
_____
_____

That IS happiness!

Day 79

Do you see fresh or rotten tomatoes? Because that determines your experience.

I invite you to find all the fresh tomatoes in your life - the positive, loving, fun, joyous, peaceful, and phenomenal - and focus on them. Then make a huge list!

That IS happiness!

Day 80

Imagine a soft and gentle blanket. Picture yourself touching it.

How does this feel? Pampering, cozy, nice? Write about this gentle energy to shift yourself into your own soft spot; your heart. BE and live your new day from that beautiful space.

That IS happiness!

Day 81

Gain clarity with a YES or NO day! That is a day where no "maybe," no "probably," no "perhaps," and certainly no "I don't know" phrases have any space to even exist.

What in your life is a clear NO? What is a clear YES? All maybe, probably, perhaps, and I don't knows equal a NO for now—no decision is made on those, to be asked again at a later time. Feel into your NO's and YESes, how do they feel? Make a list to gain incredible clarity of what works and what doesn't and become acquainted with your true YES and NO.

_____
_____
_____
_____
_____
_____
_____
_____
_____
_____
_____
_____
_____
_____

That IS happiness!

Day 82

Imagine eating a spoon full of ice cream!

What words would you use to describe the taste, your feelings, and your thoughts? And for inspirational sake, "Do you want more of these brilliant feelings?" How will you create an abundance of such well-feeling moments in your new day? How can you experience your life more consciously in every "normal" moment—like eating your ice cream?

_____

That IS happiness!

Day 83

Where does your power lay? How many of the unfitting happenings in your life are really your doing? And how many of them are someone else's doing with you simply caught in the middle of it?

List all of these happenings, specifying "mine" or "not mine." How can you shift the "mine" ones into being a better experience for you and claiming your power to change your life? Is accepting, respecting, appreciating, thanking, and loving them anyways in the cards? Or is changing them radically better? How will you let the "not mine" go for good and forever? In meditation, by journaling, or imagining flushing them down the toilet with a nice wave goodbye?

That IS happiness!

Day 84

Imagine you have pizza dough in your hands! This dough is ready to be formed into a pizza shape. First you stretch it slowly in every direction. Then you stretch it more and more, farther and farther. Because you know that the more you stretch it, the smoother it gets, and the better the pizza dough will bake and taste.

How will you stretch and mold your physical body like that pizza dough in your hands—so your physical body is more flexible and living your life feels better?

_____
_____
_____
_____
_____
_____
_____
_____
_____
_____
_____
_____
_____
_____

That IS happiness!

Day 85

Clean out!

What will you clean out today? Your home and material things, un-fitting happenings in your life, thoughts that don't feel good, or feelings of lower frequency? Write your cleansing list and start cleaning out!

_____
_____
_____
_____
_____
_____
_____
_____
_____
_____
_____
_____
_____
_____
_____
_____
_____
_____
_____
_____

That IS happiness!

Day 86

Imagine yourself smiling while jumping on a trampoline.

How does that feel? Happy? What are your thoughts while jumping? Creative and playful ones, or none at all—like a meditative state? How can you jump from joy to joy - like you would jump from trampoline to trampoline - while filling yourself with bliss with every new jump you take?

That IS happiness!

Day 87

Visualize your physical life as a garden that you get to design and seed as you like!

Having an unlimited amount of - and infinite choices in - seeds, all the time you could wish for to nourish them, and complete power over what you want to grow in your garden, what will you plant? Anger, resentment, sadness or happiness, bliss, abundance and health? How will you weed out what you don't want? Journal about your perfect life-garden!

That IS happiness!

Day 88

Imagine a perfect resting place for you! It can be a nice big bed, a quiet space in the woods, a sauna, or a boat on the ocean. Use the first picture that comes to your mind. Observe your resting place!

Very descriptively write how your wonderful space looks and feels—breathe into it. Go there often during your new day!

That IS happiness!

Day 89

Imagine that this is what happens when you walk up the stairs:

- ***With every step you take, you walk up and forward in what you want, and up and closer to yourself.***
- ***With every stair you climb, you go higher and higher in your life. The higher you get, the happier you get.***
- ***With every floor landing you reach, you get to leave something non-fitting behind. A happy good-bye indeed.***

Getting closer to yourself, feeling higher and happier, and letting go more often—how does that feel? How will you take the stair approach today?

_____
_____
_____
_____
_____
_____
_____
_____
_____

That IS happiness!

Day 90

Imagine that in your new day all you can see, hear, taste, smell, feel, and think is the word "calm."

Do you feel calm yet? What does calm mean to you? How does it feel to be calm, and what are your thoughts when you are calm? Write it down calmly.

_____
_____
_____
_____
_____
_____
_____
_____
_____
_____
_____
_____
_____
_____
_____
_____
_____
_____
_____
_____

That IS happiness!

Day 91

Think of the monkey bars at a playground! You swing forward from bar to bar, hanging on tight with at least one hand until you have a firm grip on the following bar, then you let go and swing forward to the next. And so on. Do the same with your happiness!

How does it feel to be on the monkey bars? Playful, exhilarating, young, and fun? What happiness right now can you hang onto, until the next happiness stares you in the face?

_____
_____
_____
_____
_____
_____
_____
_____
_____
_____
_____
_____
_____
_____
_____
_____

That IS happiness!

Day 92

Imagine that you are at a play. You are seated and very excited. The play starts and the whole crowd is immediately captured by all the happenings on stage. It is a true masterpiece!

What kind of amazing play will your new day be? How will you un-notice all the little mishaps, and instead, only focus on your grand play of today?

That IS happiness!

Day 93

Washing the dishes by hand, cleaning the toilet, or getting ready for a gala are all the same! These are all experiences that are part of your physical life, and no experience has more value than the other.

What mood will you choose to be in to add the highest value possible to every moment? Is it a happy, grateful, and fun energy? Write about your intended vibe for today!

_____
_____
_____
_____
_____
_____
_____
_____
_____
_____
_____
_____
_____
_____
_____
_____
_____

That IS happiness!

Day 94

Imagine two different people walking down the street on different sides. One is simply just walking down the street. The other has a spring in their step.

Who has more fun in life right now and who shares and spreads a wonderful energy to everything and everyone? I think you can guess—so how will you make sure that you are walking with a happy spring? What feelings, thoughts, and activities will you spring through in your new day?

_____
_____
_____
_____
_____
_____
_____
_____
_____
_____
_____
_____
_____
_____
_____
_____

That IS happiness!

Day 95

Shoes!

What shoes do you have? How does wearing - or looking at - these different shoes make you feel? What shoes will match how you want to feel today? Write about your shoes! Then put on the fitting ones and if your vibe fits two pairs just climb today's stairs mismatched!

That IS happiness!

Day 96

Imagine someone spills a drink! Usually they are in distress about this happening. Now imagine that you say to them "It is OK, it is all OK. Are you OK?" Hearing these words lets them relax, maybe even gets them to smile or laugh about their mishap.

What feelings does "It's OK" initiate for you? What stressful happening can you shift into relaxation by saying to yourself, "It is OK, it is all OK, I am OK!" And who could you support with a calming, "It's OK!" today?

That IS happiness!

Day 97

Lose yourself!

In what moment can you lose yourself, and how will you lose yourself today? What is your expected outcome if you give yourself the permission to relax a little into whatever comes your way? Spontaneous surprises, magical new moments, fresh inspirations?

That IS happiness!

Day 98

Imagine that you and your physical body are hanging out for a chat with a cup of tea. Next imagine that you are hanging out with your mind for a chat with a cup of tea. Then imagine that you and your soul are hanging out for a chat and a cup of tea. And lastly, imagine that you are hanging out with your consciousness for a chat with a cup of tea.

What will you talk about? What plans will you create together? What emotions, thoughts, and one-ness is coming up at teatime? Let your ideas be born!

_____
_____
_____
_____
_____
_____
_____
_____
_____
_____
_____
_____
_____
_____

That IS happiness!

Day 99

Be a rebel!

What can you solve, change, or fulfill with your rebel-ness by doing the opposite of what is? Like when you are hungry you eat, when you are sweaty you shower, or when you are tired you go to sleep. List please!

_____

That IS happiness!

Day 100

Imagine that you are skydiving!

Besides being an incredible adventure that is exhilarating to no end - I did it and loved it - this act takes a lot of trust. Without it, one would never do it. What is trust to you? How does it feel? What can you trust newly, or trust again?

___

That IS happiness!

Day 101

Light a candle!

I n that sacred light, choose a mantra that is dearest to your heart. Put it here to remember!

_____
_____
_____
_____
_____
_____
_____
_____
_____
_____
_____
_____
_____
_____
_____
_____
_____
_____
_____
_____
_____

That IS happiness!

Day 102

Imagine your own happiness garden!

What does your happiness garden look and feel like—what colors are present? What people, animals, and situations fit in this sacred you-space? How do you feel when you stand in the middle of it? Journal about your magical happiness garden!

That IS happiness!

Day 103

Being generous is a world changer!

What is generosity for you? How does it feel and what thoughts match those emotions? What kind of generosity can you give, and also receive, today? Hugs, love, smiles?

That IS happiness!

Day 104

Imagine you have two ponds. One is full of water lilies, while the other has only a few. Your friendly neighbor asks if you could share some with them, for their pond. You say yes. Which pond will you take them from? The one that is full of lilies, so it won't matter if you take some out? Or the pond with only a few, which would make it look empty?

How can you make sure that your pond is always full before you share yourself? What kind of self-care can you give to yourself—to make sure you are filled with energy, health, joy, and well-feeling at all times?

That IS happiness!

Day 105

Tune-in to your magic channel! Detach from everyone's hurrying and let it all pass beside you.

How can you slow down so you have time to live in your magic channel—where experiencing all there is for you, right now and right here, is easy? How does it feel to tune-in to your magic channel? Peaceful, restful, and wonderful?

That IS happiness!

Day 106

Imagine letting your little sibling have the last cookie in the jar, even though you want it. You smile and indulge in the happiness your sibling is expressing with getting that last cookie. This shifts you to BE and live in a high-for-life frequency, because it is a magnanimous act! The word magnanimous means "great soul." It carries the energy of big-hearted, noble, and generous.

What noble and generous moments of such grandness will you create for yourself in your new day? How can you act big-hearted towards yourself and others?

_____
_____
_____
_____
_____
_____
_____
_____
_____
_____
_____
_____
_____

That IS happiness!

Day 107

Take every moment you can to look up into the sky! Every time, look as though you are seeing it for the first time ever. Because you are!

Look right now, what do you see? How does the sky shift you; into wonder and magic? Let your imagination and feelings explode—put them onto paper!

That IS happiness!

Day 108

Imagine a flower in the wind! It moves a little to the right, a little to the left, a little backward, a little forward. All with the wind! And even though there is a lot of shifting, the flower does not break. It seems that the flower has enough trust in itself to be flexible and strong enough, to bend and spring back.

How can you, and will you, bend with what is going on in your life right now? Put it into words—end with "Nothing can break me!" Breathe into that!

_____
_____
_____
_____
_____
_____
_____
_____
_____
_____
_____
_____
_____
_____
_____

That IS happiness!

Day 109

BE gigantically open!

What situation, people, and happening will you be completely open to today? Anything that is new, old, or repeating—what amazing experiences will you freely allow?

That IS happiness!

Day 110

Imagine you are walking on a path along the side of a beautiful and adventurous river. Suddenly there is a luxurious boat filled with energies of love, beauty, abundance, positivity, happiness, and health pulling right up next to you.

How does that feel? What are your thoughts? What do you want to do—hop on, look at it, or let it pass? Write this adventurous story of yours!

_____
_____
_____
_____
_____
_____
_____
_____
_____
_____
_____
_____
_____
_____
_____
_____
_____
_____

That IS happiness!

Day 111

You are a shiner! Shiners are people that shine their light bright no matter what is happening for them!

How will you shine your light bright and strong no matter the circumstances—for yourself and others? Will you smile, laugh, and compliment all day long? Will you align with your love and spread it far and wide?

That IS happiness!

Day 112

Imagine an ever-moving squirrel!

How can you be a squirrel—flexible, active, playful, and full of movement? How can you have such fun today? Make your squirrel-plan below!

_____
_____
_____
_____
_____
_____
_____
_____
_____
_____
_____
_____
_____
_____
_____
_____
_____
_____
_____

That IS happiness!

Day 113

Kindness changes everything!

What is kindness for you? How does kindness feel? What kind of kindness can you give today? What kindness can you allow yourself to receive?

That IS happiness!

Day 114

Imagine that you get to pick a super-power!

What super-power would you wish for? And how will you use it, for yourself and others?

That IS happiness!

Day 115

In any great working community, if one component is in an uneasy state, the other components who are feeling great take over, help out, and balance everything.

How can you create a healthy community in your whole being and with your surroundings? What goodness will you do for your physical body, mind, soul, and consciousness today?

That IS happiness!

Day 116

Imagine someone standing at a street corner saying, "Thank you!" to everyone and everything passing by.

How do the words "Thank you!" make you feel—giving and receiving? Who could you say "Thank you!" to more often? Yourself? How can you say the best ever "Thank you!" to yourself and others today?

That IS happiness!

Day 117

Just as a house gets dusty and dirty and is in need of cleaning, your energy becomes impure and needs cleaning too.

What wonderful energy cleaning practices will you do today? Breathe consciously, be mindful, sit with a candle, feel your heart and love, meditate, laugh and smile a lot? Make your purifying list!

That IS happiness!

Day 118

Imagine a falcon! Even though it is presented with opportunities to hunt and eat in every split second of its life, the falcon will not take every single one. Because hunting like a crazy bird would be exhausting, and it would be too much food. It only hunts when it is ready, hungry, or simply can't resist because it feels right and good.

How can you copy the powerful focus of a falcon into your new day—and only go for the nourishing opportunities and experiences?

_____
_____
_____
_____
_____
_____
_____
_____
_____
_____
_____
_____
_____
_____

That IS happiness!

Day 119

"I say YES!"

How does that sound to you, and what feelings do you have when you say, "I say YES!"? What will you say yes to in your new day and what will you say yes to more often? Yes-sayer list please!

That IS happiness!

Day 120

Imagine that you are looking at a field of lush green grass.

How does this feel for you? What does the color green and this beautiful nature visualization activate in you? Peace, happiness, spaciousness? Feel, write, and feel some more!

That IS happiness!

Day 121

What can you fall in love with today?

Write plentifully and don't forget to list yourself!

That IS happiness!

Day 122

Imagine you inherit a pair of pants from a loved one. They fit size-wise, but oh goodness, the color and pattern is totally not you.

What inherited but un-fitting stuff will you not wear in your new day? What feelings, thoughts, and experiences will you let go? What new and fitting pants will you wear—powerful, unstoppable, and uniquely fitted-for-you ones?

_____
_____
_____
_____
_____
_____
_____
_____
_____
_____
_____
_____
_____
_____
_____
_____
_____
_____

That IS happiness!

Day 123

Celebrate a clarity-creating relationship with your opinions!

Which of your opinions feel good, and which ones do not? How can you shift the negative ones to be positive? What opinions can you celebrate as your best and finest ones? Make your opinionated list!

That IS happiness!

Day 124

Imagine you get to hug an animal that you have always wanted to hug, but normally could not.

What animal would that be? A lion, a kitten, or a monkey? What energetic qualities does your animal have? For example, a lion is very majestic. How does it feel to hug your chosen dream animal and how can you shift to be its energetic quality too?

That IS happiness!

Day 125

Twirl your way to happiness! Stand with your feet shoulder width apart, arms stretched out to your side, and fingers spread wide. Give it your flashiest smile and let's go! Twirl!

Write about the magical feeling this activity initiates in and for you. Do you feel lighter, cleaner, or more energized? Who could you twirl with today?

That IS happiness!

Day 126

Imagine yourself taking a huge bite of your favorite food!

What food is it? What wonderful and delicious sound will you make while enjoying it? "Mmmmmmm..." perhaps? How does this devouring and food-sounding feel for you? Happy?

That IS happiness!

Day 127

Close your eyes, smile, and listen in stillness!

What sounds do you hear? What messages will you listen to in your new day—the signs of your body, the voices of your thoughts and feelings? Your loved ones? Make your "I'm a good listener" list!

That IS happiness!

Day 128

Imagine that you are a warrior!

How do you feel as your warrior? How do you move and think—what do you choose, being that power? How will you live your new day as your unstoppable warrior energy?

That IS happiness!

Day 129

Finding comfort is key!

How does comfort look and feel to you? What kind of different comfort can you find and create for yourself today? How can you serve others by giving comfort to them?

That IS happiness!

Day 130

Imagine pouring your whole life through a colander, like with pasta that is done cooking.

What will be left once you have sifted your whole life? Because that's the goodness, just like the pasta, that you want to experience and digest. List your bounty and focus on that!

___

That IS happiness!

Day 131

The gift of a visitor! Think of a loved one calling you, saying "Hey, I have a few days off and I want to come visit. Is it beautiful where you live? What do you love about it, and why would it be an amazing place for me to visit, other than because you are there?"

What would you say—it's wonderful? What would you mention; your favorite park, an amazing restaurant, your nice home, or the breathtaking sunset? How can you see your life and where you live through the eyes of a visitor today?

_____
_____
_____
_____
_____
_____
_____
_____
_____
_____
_____
_____
_____

That IS happiness!

Day 132

Imagine yourself standing in front of a mirror! See yourself and say: "I accept, respect, appreciate, thank, and love myself completely and wholeheartedly; with all my ups and downs, my lefts and rights, and my forwards and backwards including my twists of anger, sadness, happiness, quirkiness, and uniqueness. I love all of me!"

I say, go do it for real! Find the nearest mirror and gush about yourself, to yourself. Look at yourself! What are the most amazingly wonderful words you can shower yourself with? What lovingness will you say?

_____
_____
_____
_____
_____
_____
_____
_____
_____
_____
_____
_____
_____
_____
_____

That IS happiness!

Day 133

You, others, every word and sound, every smell and taste, every thought and feeling, and every happening are all vibrating energy. And vibrating means it is moving. You can play with that movement!

What in your life would you like to move around, or change? How can you play with that energy, shifting it from a lower frequency - anger, frustration, or sadness - to a higher one like gratitude, hope, and love?

_____
_____
_____
_____
_____
_____
_____
_____
_____
_____
_____
_____
_____
_____
_____

That IS happiness!

Day 134

Your pain is your best friend! It never lies to you, it is straight up in your face, and it lets you know without hesitation that you are lost and not in your middle. It keeps you honest when you don't love yourself, and it is a great chit-chatter that loves to communicate and answer questions for you. It does all that because it loves you!

Where is your pain right now? Start asking it questions! What is it telling you—what wisdom does it hold and what guidance does it have for you? Most importantly, what actions does it tell you to take?

_____
_____
_____
_____
_____
_____
_____
_____
_____
_____
_____
_____
_____
_____
_____

That IS happiness!

Day 135

Imagine that you are running your own business. Your business has many different employees who bring their best every day in order to make your company an abundance-filled experience. In return, you show them acceptance, respect, appreciation, thankfulness, and love. Your physical body is your business! You have many organs in your body, and they bring their best, every single day, in order to make life in your body an abundance-filled experience.

How will you accept, respect, appreciate, thank, and love your body, and all your organs, today?

_____
_____
_____
_____
_____
_____
_____
_____
_____
_____
_____
_____
_____
_____

That IS happiness!

Day 136

Bless everything and everyone you feel you are having trouble with!

Bless all the *what*—happenings, situations, and things. How will you do that? And bless all the *who*—people, people, and more people. How will you do that?

That IS happiness!

Day 137

Imagine breathing in light that is in the color of your choice! Make sure you choose one that shifts you to BE and live in your high-for-life frequency. Then breathe out, and let go of all un-loving, un-fitting, unhappy feelings, and thoughts that you have.

What color is your favorite—how does it make you feel? Breathe into this! What will you let go of?

_____
_____
_____
_____
_____
_____
_____
_____
_____
_____
_____
_____
_____
_____
_____
_____

That IS happiness!

Day 138

Make some important decisions that will carry and support you throughout your new day. Say or think "I decide to…!"

List all your intentions that will empower you to BE and live in your truth today! Then it's rehearsing time.

_____
_____
_____
_____
_____
_____
_____
_____
_____
_____
_____
_____
_____
_____
_____
_____
_____
_____
_____
_____
_____

That IS happiness!

Day 139

Pick something or someone you think very highly of! It could be a family member, friend, historical figure, or something like the sky, moon, sun, or an animal.

Why do you think so highly of them—what is the admired quality? Pause for a minute and make a list! Take this admiration-list and say, "I have that same quality, I admire_____in myself too."

That IS happiness!

Day 140

Imagine you are standing at the gate of an incredible huge nature park. You are so excited to see, smell, taste, hear, think, and feel all of the plants, animals, birds, and scenery in there. You enter, and it is already breathtaking; you are in awe. You walk about 100 steps further into the park, then stop. You look to the left and to the right, and then turn around. You think, "That was great!" and then you leave out through the gate, back home.

Do you think going further into that park and staying for a while would have made this experience more impressive? How much more vivid could you experience your life by going deeper and further into it?

That IS happiness!

Day 141

Think of a radar speed sign blinking like crazy because you are driving too fast! When you see it blinking you check your speed and naturally slow down. With that, you become more aware of yourself and your doings; your car and everything around you. It shifts you into your now!

How can you slow down in your new day? What happenings can you slow down or even bring to a stand-still for today?

That IS happiness!

Day 142

Imagine that you are meeting your NOW for a cup of tea and some chit-chat.

What will you say to your NOW? What will your NOW say to you? How can you put more gloriousness into your NOW? How can you love your NOW more? Most importantly, how can you pull yourself into your NOW in a more focused way?

That IS happiness!

Day 143

Remember!

What energy, feelings, and thoughts does the word *remember* initiate for you—nostalgia, a slow down, an alignment? What well-feeling essence could you remember more today; love, happiness, peace?

_____
_____
_____
_____
_____
_____
_____
_____
_____
_____
_____
_____
_____
_____
_____
_____
_____
_____

That IS happiness!

Day 144

Imagine a child, so super excited and "over the moon" happy that they squeeze their shoulders up and together, make little fists in front of their chest, pull their chin down a bit, smile, and shake with excitement.

How does that feel for you—now and when you were that child? How can you create this type of happiness, playfulness, and excitement for yourself? Over-the-moon-happiness-list please!

_____
_____
_____
_____
_____
_____
_____
_____
_____
_____
_____
_____
_____
_____
_____
_____

That IS happiness!

Day 145

Rejuvenating your energy is an important puzzle piece to be happy; just as eating clean food, sleeping a deep sleep, and exercising to stay fit is.

What does rejuvenation feel like for you? Beautiful, relaxed, healthy? How will you regenerate your body, mind, soul, and consciousness today?

That IS happiness!

Day 146

"Come on and do the twist…"

What does a twist represent to you? Fun, play, flexibility, youthfulness? What can you twist today, your mood? How will you twist your body, mind, soul, and consciousness to shift yourself to well-feeling? Who could you twist with in your new day?

That IS happiness!

Day 147

Think of a big house with a basement, first, second, third, fourth, fifth, and sixth floor. Every floor is one room, one window, and represents one phase of your life. The basement is before birth. The first floor is your baby time. The second is your toddler phase. The third is your childhood. The fourth your teenage phase. The fifth is your young adult time, and the sixth floor is your NOW.

Go to every floor and feel yourself into a happy and wished-for version of every phase in your life. Important—leave the yucky stuff out. Write these blissful visions down and breathe into them.

That IS happiness!

Day 148

Imagine you are making a delicious "life-smoothie" for your new day!

What feelings, activities, thoughts, words, and happenings go into that delicious life smoothie—love, the peaceful color green, a bubble bath, or music and dancing? Recipe please!

That IS happiness!

Day 149

Is it your perfect cup of coffee, or is it not?

Ask that question about what and who is in your life right now. The perfect ones, enjoy fully. The no's, ask what plan of action is better: making the best of it, moving on, or happily create a new and better cup of coffee?

That IS happiness!

Day 150

Support your decisions!

What decisions made by you in the past can you support in a better way—because to be fair, at the time, you chose what you believed to be best? What decisions will you finally celebrate with worthiness—setting yourself free while you're at it?

_____
_____
_____
_____
_____
_____
_____
_____
_____
_____
_____
_____
_____
_____
_____
_____
_____
_____
_____
_____

That IS happiness!

Day 151

Cultivating a pure heart is just as important as cultivating pure water. If your water would be dirty and cloudy, you would filter it until it was clean, clear, and as pure as you can get it to be.

What will you do to cleanse your heart today? Loving self-care, well-feeling activities, meditation? What will you focus on to keep your love-producing center as pure as possible in your new day?

That IS happiness!

Day 152

Imagine a chef's kitchen at a five-star hotel. Every single person working in that kitchen is playing an important part to make it a high-end restaurant. Together they succeed and co-create an outstanding place to dine.

What beautiful co-creation with other people and the world will you make happen in your new day? What mood will you show up as, to ensure a creation of magic and success?

That IS happiness!

Day 153

Colors are a great tool to shift yourself to wellness!

What is your perfect wellness color for today? How does it make you feel? Where will you find it—in your clothing, surroundings, food, or elsewhere?

That IS happiness!

Day 154

Imagine you create your garden for your new day. You plant it with your thoughts, intentions, wishes, dreams, and your to-do list. Put all you have into your gardening skills and make it a spectacular garden for you to enjoy all day long.

How will your wonderful and well-feeling garden look and feel? How will you stay in your own garden today? How will you know when you have left to go into someone else's garden—is it a feeling of unhappiness or restlessness?

_____
_____
_____
_____
_____
_____
_____
_____
_____
_____
_____
_____
_____
_____
_____
_____

That IS happiness!

Day 155

Your NOW and your FORWARD go hand in hand! Your NOW is where all your power lays. FORWARD is the way you want everything to go in order to grow, develop, and change.

How is your NOW and how will you stay present in your NOW? How can you chose your phenomenal FORWARD and feel excited for your next?

_____
_____
_____
_____
_____
_____
_____
_____
_____
_____
_____
_____
_____
_____
_____
_____
_____

That IS happiness!

Day 156

Imagine you are at a store. You are finished with what you came to get and decide it is time to leave. In other words, you are ready to move on, because where you are at is not fitting anymore. You pay, find the exit, step through it, and enter into the outside. By exiting, you let go or leave behind all that was in that store and move on into your new.

What things, happenings, and people will you let go of every time you leave a store—or even better, leave any place through a door?

That IS happiness!

Day 157

When gentle becomes a healing opportunity!

What is gentle for you? How does it feel? What gentle-ness do you have inside of you, and where does it live—in your heart? What gentle thoughts do you want to think more often? How can you create gentleness for yourself and others today?

_____
_____
_____
_____
_____
_____
_____
_____
_____
_____
_____
_____
_____
_____
_____
_____
_____
_____

That IS happiness!

Day 158

Your new day is like a spa with many opportunities to feel pampered!

How can you create a spa environment for yourself in your new day? How can you energize, hydrate, refresh and rejuvenate, practice color-wellness, relax, nourish, spark happiness, feel awakened and pampered, and be perfumed today? So many opportunities, make your spa-list!

That IS happiness!

Day 159

To have an upward day, you have to live in an upward frequency!

What does *upward* feel like for you—better, higher, freer? What *upward* thoughts and feelings can you focus on today? What upward-ness in your surroundings can you notice; stairs, elevators?

That IS happiness!

Day 160

Visualize your beautiful light!

You are a light! Close your eyes and breathe into your light, welcome it. How does it feel—is it big or small, white or colored, bright or dim? Write about your light, and take whatever sense you get a notch or two up. More really is better here!

That IS happiness!

Day 161

There is a position open. Your life is looking for a leader. Interested?

What does it mean for you to be the leader of your life? How interested are you in this "perfect for you" position? Use strong adjectives and words here!

That IS happiness!

Day 162

Imagine you are at a ball, all dressy and fancy. You are smiling, dancing, and enjoying your wonderful time. A pure high-for-life experience.

How does that feel, special, amazing? How will you stay in a well-feeling essence - like being at this ball - in your new day, no matter what or who of lesser joy comes into your awareness?

That IS happiness!

Day 163

Stop and look no further!

Write about all the magic that is there for you right now! No looking backward, forward, or to the side—only right here and now.

That IS happiness!

Day 164

Imagine a strawberry!

What does a strawberry initiate for you—colorful? Playful? Happy? Juicy and sweet? Or pick another favorite fruit—what goodness does this favorite fruit make you feel, think, taste, see, smell, or think of? Write to shift yourself into a blissful frequency, then stay there all day long!

That IS happiness!

Day 165

What energy are you creating for yourself right now? What you think, feel, see, hear, taste, and smell is all energy. Depending on its nature you fill every single cell of your body, mind, soul, and consciousness with either good feeling energy or not good feeling energy. Which then determines how you feel, good or not good.

Is your energy good or not so good? Become aware, then ask yourself, "How can I improve my energy right now?" Journal about how you want to feel and how you can make that happen.

_____
_____
_____
_____
_____
_____
_____
_____
_____
_____
_____
_____
_____
_____
_____

That IS happiness!

Day 166

Imagine that you are sitting somewhere and start tapping your feet to a beat.

How cool and good do you feel doing this? Use your most wonderful words to describe this fun feeling—then go be that fun all day long!

That IS happiness!

Day 167

Chit-chat with what you find! Everyone always finds something. Sometimes it's a leaf, a penny, feather, a piece of paper with a word or saying on it, or a piece of glitter.

I invite you to chat with what you find! What questions will you ask? For example, ask a leaf blowing by because it knows the way; a raindrop because it knows all about flow; or a penny because it's a teacher of abundance. Silly or not silly, list it all!

_____
_____
_____
_____
_____
_____
_____
_____
_____
_____
_____
_____
_____
_____
_____
_____

That IS happiness!

Day 168

Become a programmer and program your breath to be a nutritious message for your whole being!

What nourishing thoughts and feelings can you imprint into your breathing of in and out today? In comes love, out goes the gunk?

_____
_____
_____
_____
_____
_____
_____
_____
_____
_____
_____
_____
_____
_____
_____
_____
_____
_____
_____

That IS happiness!

Day 169

When you decide to take a road trip, you choose a desired destination, plan the route, check the car, and the weather. You prepare and pack. Time to go!

Looking at your new day as a road trip that has unplanned things happening. How can you plan ahead, yet still stay flexible and relaxed?

___
___
___
___
___
___
___
___
___
___
___
___
___
___
___
___
___
___
___
___

That IS happiness!

Day 170

Imagine yourself breathing and doing nothing!

If you can, really do that in your new day! How delicious do you feel in that nothing-ness? How many times will you allow yourself to hang out in this empty, yet so full, space today?

That IS happiness!

Day 171

"You are amazing!"

Say, think, and write this truthful sentence to yourself! How does this feel? Are you smiling? Say it to others too—how are they reacting? Say it about your life and watch it shift!

That IS happiness!

Day 172

Imagine that every time you open your hands, they fill with lots of confetti infused with high-for-life feelings you wish to spread. Once filled, you throw those pieces high up into the air. On their way back down they bless everything and everyone they encounter with the goodness of these infusions. Then they dissolve into Mother Earth, nourishing and blessing her too, sharing this goodness with the whole universe.

What feelings are in these confetti pieces? Love, hope, wellbeing? Who will you spread them to today? Yourself, others - names please - and Earth?

_____
_____
_____
_____
_____
_____
_____
_____
_____
_____
_____
_____

That IS happiness!

Day 173

Joy, joyous, joyously, joyousness, joyful, joy-filled… jump for joy!

What is joy for you? How does it feel? How will you make sure to BE and live joyously today?

_____
_____
_____
_____
_____
_____
_____
_____
_____
_____
_____
_____
_____
_____
_____
_____
_____
_____
_____

That IS happiness!

Day 174

Imagine having the power of super glue!

What does the power of super glue feel like for you? What feelings, thoughts, happenings, and joy do you want to be glued to today? Love, positivity, and fun activities? List please!

_____
_____
_____
_____
_____
_____
_____
_____
_____
_____
_____
_____
_____
_____
_____
_____
_____
_____
_____
_____
_____

That IS happiness!

Day 175

Fierceness and power!

You have it too, everyone does! What fierceness do you have in you, on you, as you, maybe even around you? Is it your eyes or voice, your determination or clarity, your love or bliss?

That IS happiness!

Day 176

Imagine that you are standing in front of your brand new house.

How does it feel? Are you in awe that you get to live in this amazing place? Write it down! Your house is your whole you in this—your physical body, mind, soul, and consciousness. What is it like to feel that amazing about your brand new you?

That IS happiness!

Day 177

Your TV remote control is a powerful device!

Having such a channel changing power in your hands, what channel will you choose - or change to - in your new day? Happy, interesting, a channel with a rich program?

That IS happiness!

Day 178

Imagine that there is this problem you have.

Without going in too deeply, how will you embrace your issues today? How will you love and thank them? How will you invite them to stay as long as needed—to receive the full gift of their visit?

That IS happiness!

Day 179

Break the universal record of making yourself, everyone, and everything feel amazing about themselves!

How can you uplift yourself and others today? What words match that intent? What thoughts are you going to focus on? Will you smile while breaking this great record?

_____
_____
_____
_____
_____
_____
_____
_____
_____
_____
_____
_____
_____
_____
_____
_____
_____

That IS happiness!

Day 180

Imagine you and your loved ones are in a nice restaurant. You get served delicious food presented like art. You are excited and hungry, and you feel amazing and happy. But then you notice a hair in your food! Yikes!

How will you not let anything or anyone get in between you and your enjoyment of being in this nice place—in your nice new day?

_____
_____
_____
_____
_____
_____
_____
_____
_____
_____
_____
_____
_____
_____
_____
_____
_____

That IS happiness!

Day 181

Visualize and feel ahead!

How do you want to feel today? What kind of day do you want to have? What are your visions ahead?

That IS happiness!

Day 182

Imagine that you have a love tank, a happiness tank, a nutrition tank, a sleep tank, a peace tank, etc.

How will you keep these tanks full and refilled in your new day? What kind of love, happiness, nutrition, sleep, and peace practices can you gift yourself?

That IS happiness!

Day 183

Life is an ever changing and moving experience, and sometimes it changes faster than you can create differently.

What can you simply let be as-is, while trusting that change will happen anyways? Where can you back off and, instead, open your heart and embrace what is?

That IS happiness!

Day 184

Imagine that you are going on a walk and notice a sign that reads, "Please keep this area clean!"

What area in your life will you clean - and keep clean - of unwell feelings today? Who will you show the sign of "Keep my area clean!" to?

That IS happiness!

Day 185

Start a high-for-life frequency journal!

This should be a piece of cake for you, since you have been doing this from Day 1 of this workbook! Write down everything in and on you that you love. Your heart, your smile, your pinky toe—put it on this wonderful list! Scribble about who and what makes you feel happy—everything and everyone that is "high-for-life" counts!

_____
_____
_____
_____
_____
_____
_____
_____
_____
_____
_____
_____
_____
_____
_____
_____
_____

That IS happiness!

Day 186

Imagine that you are at the beach using a metal detector. You are scanning every inch of sand to find metal.

Scan your whole being without judgment—how do you feel in your physical body, mind, soul, and in your consciousness? Feel the awareness you are gaining here!

That IS happiness!

Day 187

What kind of water do you need right now? Water is a spectacular delivery source of flowing, clean, moving, clear, detoxing, alive, and refreshing energy.

Describe what water you would enjoy right now—what energy is best for you at this moment. Is it bubbly, still, naturally colored or flavored, fruity, sweet, or all natural?

_____
_____
_____
_____
_____
_____
_____
_____
_____
_____
_____
_____
_____
_____
_____
_____
_____
_____
_____

That IS happiness!

Day 188

Imagine you are en-route on a road trip. At some point you stop to look where you are, and what time it is. You smile and say "Great! I am exactly where I am supposed to be."

How will you make sure that on this road trip of a new day you feel that wherever you are is exactly where you are supposed to be? A mantra, sticky notes all over your house that say "I am exactly where I am supposed to be," or aligning with your journey through meditation?

That IS happiness!

Day 189

Your beautiful mouth does a lot! It does more than just show off your amazing lips, carry your powerful teeth, or be the gate for your wonderful voice to come to life through. Used properly, it can immediately lift and shift your energy into happiness through exercise and silliness.

Smile! How does that feel? Frown, how does that feel? How can you guarantee that you will smile more often today? Set a smile alarm once an hour?

That IS happiness!

Day 190

Imagine you are at a store buying a cookie. You choose the cookie that looks best to you by believing it is delicious.

How do you feel in this act of believing—happy? Knowing? So totally sure? What new or old beliefs can you nourish to be of the same sweetness like your cookie-buying one?

_____
_____
_____
_____
_____
_____
_____
_____
_____
_____
_____
_____
_____
_____
_____
_____
_____

That IS happiness!

Day 191

ME for me, and only then with everyone together!

Sounds selfish, but is it? What ME for ME activities, words, feelings, thoughts, and pampering will you do today to make sure that your ME tank is full - and overflowing - so you show up as the best you that you can be?

That IS happiness!

Day 192

Imagine that you are in your car listening to the radio and a person calls into the station, winning a trip to Paris. Wow! The caller's overjoyed reaction and the excitement created by the radio studio is absolutely spectacular. That powerful joy is energy, and it has the ability to overflow to each and everyone listening. YOU!

What experience in your life - or in someone else's life - is of such an incredible exciting and alive magnitude for you to latch onto?

_____
_____
_____
_____
_____
_____
_____
_____
_____
_____
_____
_____
_____
_____
_____

That IS happiness!

Day 193

Remember when, as a child, you played on without end - happy and worry free - and how when it was time to stop playing, your frown and un-happiness were unleashed until you could play again?

How can you be that playful right now—so when playtime is over, you'll miss it? What activities, people to play with, music to dance to, or places to visit go on your list?

_____
_____
_____
_____
_____
_____
_____
_____
_____
_____
_____
_____
_____
_____
_____
_____

That IS happiness!

Day 194

Picture a stopwatch! You start it, you stop it, you reset it, and then have a fresh go.

What un-fitting situation can you stop, reset, and start fresh in your life right now?

That IS happiness!

Day 195

Pick a person who inspires and really impresses you. Someone you think the world of. If I ask you to tell me why you think so highly of them, you would reflect on their whole person, lives, happenings, and doings. You would list all they have accomplished and experienced and base your admiration on that.

Turn the spotlight onto yourself now! What about yourself impresses you? List all your accomplishments, experiences, and reflections of your whole being and your life. Focus on thinking the world of yourself!

_____
_____
_____
_____
_____
_____
_____
_____
_____
_____
_____
_____
_____
_____

That IS happiness!

Day 196

Imagine that you are standing in a delicious ice cream parlor wanting ice cream really bad. But, there you are looking at your phone in search for an ice cream parlor out there. Sounds silly, right?

What are you searching for in your outer-world that is actually in your inner-world—is it peace, love, respect, satisfaction, happiness? Have a close thought and make your list!

_____
_____
_____
_____
_____
_____
_____
_____
_____
_____
_____
_____
_____
_____
_____
_____

That IS happiness!

Day 197

Beautify your new day!

What feelings come up for you with the words beauty, beautiful, and beautifying—graciousness, nature, love and light? How does this shift you? How will you beautify your today and focus on this well-feeling?

That IS happiness!

Day 198

Imagine your perfect comfort zone!

How does that feel; familiar, normal? Now imagine leaving it to go on an adventure, to experience exciting new-ness. How does that feel? Where and how will you leave your comfort zone today—to allow new-ness?

That IS happiness!

Day 199

Start an adventurous pact with your NOW! Your NOW is always a guaranteed adventure because it is constantly new, updated, and filled with new opportunities for you.

How will you make sure to be present in your wonderful NOW—set a be-present alarm once an hour? Do meditation, walk in nature, or stare at the sky?

That IS happiness!

Day 200

Imagine that you are taking a class, and that there is a vase of beautiful flowers next to the speaker. You are mesmerized by them and can't stop looking; admiring and gushing about the flowers, the colors, and the energy they carry and spread to everyone - and everything - in the room.

How beautiful are those flowers? What is so wonderful about them? How does their magic make you feel? Journal about these flowers, then realize that you have all these amazing qualities too! Breathe into that glorious fact!

_____
_____
_____
_____
_____
_____
_____
_____
_____
_____
_____
_____
_____

That IS happiness!

Day 201

You are always supported!

What is support for you? How does it feel? Where can you feel the support in your new day, from yourself? From leaning on a wall, sitting on a chair? Your feet, your physical body? The sun, the ground? The water you drink? People around you? Make your support list!

That IS happiness!

Day 202

Imagine eating an orange that has no taste! You would eat and get nutrition out of it, but not the pleasure of tasting it. That would make eating only half of the experience it is, right?

What in your life are you experiencing like that orange without taste; your physicality, your emotional state, your thoughts, or your soul essence? What in your new day will you embrace with loads of taste—with all the vividness there is?

_____
_____
_____
_____
_____
_____
_____
_____
_____
_____
_____
_____
_____
_____
_____
_____
_____
_____

That IS happiness!

Day 203

Feeling good is a high-for-life frequency!

Where in your life are you already feeling good, physically? Mentally or emotionally—at work, at home? Where do you want to feel good and what will you do to make it happen; what steps will you take to nurture this wonderful way of being and living?

That IS happiness!

Day 204

Imagine that you are having a blast while walking in a parade. You see the mass of "all" standing on the sidewalk, waving and cheering at you.

Your new day is such a parade; made of fun, goodness, wellness, and happiness, but also of un-happiness. How will you madly engage with all the good today, while leaving everything un-fitting to be part of the "everything" that make the parade?

That IS happiness!

Day 205

Remember what is important!

Feeling well! How will you create well-feeling in your physical body, your mind, your heart, and in your NOW? How will you focus on the good—in, on, and around you?

_____

That IS happiness!

Day 206

Imagine that you are vacationing at a new destination! You feel amazing, are relaxed, trusting, peaceful, happy, and open to all new. You are breathing freely and deeply. You feel curious and adventurous. Food and water tastes better than ever. You have no rules for bedtime, meal time or a dress code and have no "to do-s." Life feels easy and is a piece of cake. You smile and laugh a lot. Your body, mind, soul, and consciousness clearly are in a high-for-life frequency.

Are you thrilled, excited, and curious? How will you live your new day like you would at a new destination and on vacation—no matter if you are or not? As an idea, putting on your bathing suit could help!

_____
_____
_____
_____
_____
_____
_____
_____
_____
_____
_____

That IS happiness!

Day 207

Create a morning, mid-day, and night-time feel-good ritual!

What does your unique pampering habit look like? List some smaller, but also bigger, practices that you will gift yourself?

That IS happiness!

Day 208

Imagine that you are sitting on a comfy sofa, all relaxed and smiling. You are watching a fantastic 3D nature documentary. You feel, hear, taste, smell, think, and see all that is in this documentary very vividly—just as if you were there, but you are not! That is because this documentary is energy, connected, and shares its energy with you.

What energies will you share today, and what are the ones you wish for from others? How will you consciously celebrate one-ness with everyone and everything—with a smile and lots of laughter? With best wishes and compliments? With kindness and service?

That IS happiness!

Day 209

Pick your favorite race car! Imagine you are sitting in it and about to go drive this fabulous, powerful, and vivid car on a race car track. You are beyond excited to experience this to the fullest. You start speeding up, but soon hit the brakes.

Your old beliefs and habits are your breaks in your life, slowing your vivid physical experience way down. What are your breaks? List them, then send them off with well-wishes and your deepest love. Start racing again into your new day!

_____
_____
_____
_____
_____
_____
_____
_____
_____
_____
_____
_____
_____
_____

That IS happiness!

Day 210

Imagine that you are standing in front of a healing spa, about to go in. You are looking forward to the relaxation, recharging, cleaning, and detoxing. You take a deep breath, open the door, and step in.

What energy, hope, and wishes does going into a spa carry for you? How does being in a spa feel for you? What healing and love is initiated by you treating yourself to spa time? Breathe into this and step into your new day as you would into a spa.

_____
_____
_____
_____
_____
_____
_____
_____
_____
_____
_____
_____
_____
_____
_____
_____

That IS happiness!

Day 211

"I think I'll just be happy today!"

So simple, yet so powerful! What does this feel like for you? What inspirations are coming in by saying, thinking, and feeling this? How will you you use this potent sentence today?

That IS happiness!

Day 212

Your focus!

Where is it? Where do you want it to be? How will you shift it to your desired frequency and make sure it stays there, determinedly?

That IS happiness!

Day 213

Imagine that you are driving by a beautiful meadow filled with different wild flowers, grass, and weeds all mixed together.

Your life is that meadow—a mix of beauty and unpretty, yet, as a whole, it's beautiful. How will you center your thoughts, feelings, and experiences in the whole beauty of your wonderful life—through powerful intentions, meditation? Or through journaling?

That IS happiness!

Day 214

Go smell all of the deliciousness!

What is a delicious smell for you? How do you feel when something has a nice scent? Make a list of all wonderful fragrances and how they make you feel!

_____

That IS happiness!

Day 215

Imagine a squeaky-clean floor!

What does this clean-ness feel like for you—is it light, fresh, or new? Write about things, happenings, and people that help you to stay in such purity. Treasure them!

That IS happiness!

Day 216

Being open is a receiving way of being!

Just think of a door that's open and one that's closed; one lets in, the other keeps out. What will you open up to? Magic, solutions, betterment? How will you make sure to stay open?

That IS happiness!

Day 217

Imagine that every time you have hope, you send a magical balloon filled with positivity, uplift-tivity, betterment, intention, compassion, love, and support up into the universe.

Go on, fill those balloons! List all your hopes for yourself and others. Then let them fly high and pop to shower yourself, everyone, and everything with that glory.

___
___
___
___
___
___
___
___
___
___
___
___
___
___
___
___

That IS happiness!

Day 218

All those little messages and signs!

What are they for you? Heart-shaped things everywhere, detours saving you from traffic, a song that brings up memories, a person popping into your mind, food that steals your focus? List the ones coming up right now and keep adding new ones you notice later in the day.

___
___
___
___
___
___
___
___
___
___
___
___
___
___
___
___
___
___

That IS happiness!

Day 219

Imagine that you are lighting a candle while talking to someone and thinking about work. Once the candle is lit, you look at it for a second thinking, "That's pretty!" and then you go make dinner.

What in your life are you doing while multitasking to the maximum, but would really like to focus on more deeply to put more meaning and mindfulness into it? What are you wishing to do more consciously in your new day?

That IS happiness!

Day 220

Have you ever needed to go somewhere and do something that every cell in you simply did not agree with?

How will you make sure you get yourself into a joyful state before starting these activities, to accomplish them through your happiness? Is it by smiling first, having a good laugh before, or a sweet treat during these jobs?

That IS happiness!

Day 221

Imagine that your first thought waking up, and your last thought falling asleep, is "I am grateful!"

What does gratefulness feel like for you? How will you make sure that being grateful at every start and end of the day becomes your priority?

That IS happiness!

Day 222

Remember a time when you were "over the moon" happy!

What was the setting? How did you feel, besides being happy? What were your thoughts? Describe and re-feel this in detail. Carry this bliss with you in your new day.

_____
_____
_____
_____
_____
_____
_____
_____
_____
_____
_____
_____
_____
_____
_____
_____
_____
_____
_____
_____

That IS happiness!

Day 223

Imagine you are on a beautiful island!

How does it look, feel, smell, and taste there, and what are the sounds you hear? What are your thoughts in that paradise? Journal about this experience, while only focusing on its beauty—then go out there and live your new day from that wonderful essence of "heaven," while noticing only the good.

That IS happiness!

Day 224

Here is why you should go bake your own cake: So you are not empty-handed but have a piece to share in exchange of someone else's cake.

It's the same with your happiness! How will you create your own joy—to show up full-handed, ready to share, and multiplying your bliss while at it?

That IS happiness!

Day 225

Imagine a sky with lots of colorful balloons to take all your worries!

List all your worries, then visualize them one-by-one - or all at once - being taken away in these colorful balloons, creating a beautiful feeling and scenery for you to enjoy and admire.

___

That IS happiness!

Day 226

Find comfort in the uncomfortable!

List in what uncomfortable-ness you will find comfort today. What fear will you quiet down with lots of trust?

___

That IS happiness!

Day 227

Imagine a day where you and everyone else expects that all is well.

Feel the amazing stage this sets for your new day, then list all your well-expectations for everything and everyone including yourself. Let's call this your "all is well" list.

_____
_____
_____
_____
_____
_____
_____
_____
_____
_____
_____
_____
_____
_____
_____
_____
_____
_____
_____

That IS happiness!

Day 228

Stand proud and make it happen!

How will you make yourself visible, heard, outspoken, felt, and thought of today? How will you make space, take charge, and stand up for what you want in your new day? What will you not wait around for anymore?

That IS happiness!

Day 229

Picture how lava spreads and flows wider and wider, and farther and farther. Now imagine yourself as a whole: your body, mind, soul, and consciousness, stretching like that lava, wider and wider, and farther and father.

How does that feel? How will you spread yourself wider, grow wiser and grander, and gain new ways of being and living your truth—how will you spread into a wider territory of life, solutions, opportunities, and happenings?

That IS happiness!

Day 230

How do you pour your coffee or tea? I am going to take a real safe guess here, and say that you pour it very determinedly into a cup, instead of kind-of-sort-of point the stream of coffee or tea at the cup and loosely hit or miss.

How can you pour your energy carefully and without spilling, just like that coffee or tea? How can you avoid wasting your energy today?

_____
_____
_____
_____
_____
_____
_____
_____
_____
_____
_____
_____
_____
_____
_____
_____
_____

That IS happiness!

Day 231

Imagine that you are in a swimming pool! You don't move against the water like it's your biggest enemy, because it would get you nowhere, exhaust you, and keep you from having fun.

How can you move in and with your life in the same flowing way—relaxed, harmoniously, and floating along?

_____
_____
_____
_____
_____
_____
_____
_____
_____
_____
_____
_____
_____
_____
_____
_____

That IS happiness!

Day 232

"But why?" That is a popular and very delicate question.

Where can you stop asking this question because it slows you down, puts momentum on the unwanted, or ends your inspiration? Hint, hint—do you stop asking when wishing for change, looking at problems, or while having crazy cool ideas?

_____
_____
_____
_____
_____
_____
_____
_____
_____
_____
_____
_____
_____
_____
_____
_____
_____

That IS happiness!

Day 233

Imagine that there is a trampoline for every possible feeling you experience.

Which feeling-trampoline would you hop on, jump yourself into giggly-ness on, and revisit over and over? Make your case here, choose positively!

That IS happiness!

Day 234

Imagine a giraffe!

How would you see your life differently if you experienced it from such a height—like from a birds-eye view and an open space; less focused on the negative, and more relaxed by seeing the big picture? Be your best giraffe that you can be!

That IS happiness!

Day 235

Imagine that you are opening your eyes to your new day of happiness.

How does that feel for you? What are your thoughts in this day of happiness? How do you expect your happy day to go? Journal about your perfectly happy new day.

___

That IS happiness!

Day 236

Enjoy all your winner moments!

How does winning feel for you? Powerful, successful, accomplished, over the moon proud? What small and big winning experiences are in your life right now?

That IS happiness!

Day 237

Imagine yourself sitting on a swing.

Are you smiling yet? How can you create joyous forward swings, like excitement, to gain a higher frequency in your new day? How will you allow strengthening backwards swings like rest to fill yourself up with power today?

That IS happiness!

Day 238

Put your hand over your heart, and focus on your heart.

How does that feel? Breathe and focus on your unconditional love—for yourself, and for all. How do you feel? Wrap yourself into your own love, how does that feel? Spread your love wide—how do you feel now? Journal about what emotions this initiates for you. Enjoy!

That IS happiness!

Day 239

Imagine a huge, amazing, majestic tree completely occupied by hundreds of black birds.

How can you BE and live your own unique bird while being part of this completely occupied world? What "special" sets you apart—is your unique you? How will you align with your truth and stay aligned?

That IS happiness!

Day 240

Start a powerful and respectful companionship with your anger!

What does your anger feel like? Power? What does your anger represent for you, your inner warrior? How does a respectful relationship between you and your anger look to you? How can you embrace it with unconditional love?

_____
_____
_____
_____
_____
_____
_____
_____
_____
_____
_____
_____
_____
_____
_____
_____
_____
_____

That IS happiness!

Day 241

Imagine it is bedtime and you are about to go to sleep. The last thing you do is walk through your house, checking every room and tidying up little things here and there because you like waking up to a tidy place that welcomes you with freshness.

What similar practices can you adopt to tidy up your *energy* before going to bed? Meditation? Sitting by candle light with tea? Listen to calming music? Make your tidy-up list!

___
___
___
___
___
___
___
___
___
___
___
___
___
___

That IS happiness!

Day 242

You can ALWAYS be with yourself!

How will you "BE" with yourself today? Will a chit-chat do? Or do you need more—like meditation, quiet time, or a day off? Make a solid plan here.

_____
_____
_____
_____
_____
_____
_____
_____
_____
_____
_____
_____
_____
_____
_____
_____
_____
_____
_____
_____

That IS happiness!

Day 243

Imagine your heart as a boundless, powerful, love-rocket producing engine. Wow!

Where will you shoot these love-rockets? Where do you need this love most right now—your physical body, mind, heart, or consciousness? Who else could use some love-power? Make your "in need of love!" list!

That IS happiness!

Day 244

Being lighthearted, thinking light-mindedly, and feeling light-weighted shifts you to BE and live in a frequency of lightness.

What is light-ness for you? How does it feel, happy? Hopeful? In love? Where can you put your focus today to be light without fright?

That IS happiness!

Day 245

Imagine you get yourself something nice to drink and some delicious food. You prepare your comfy sofa with fluffy pillows and a soft blanket. You light a candle and snuggle up. You are beyond excited to observe this breathtaking movie that is about to play for you; The Story of Your Phenomenal Life!

Remember all that you have lived, felt, thought, accomplished, created, experienced, and done. Take note! Think of all your dreams, desires, and wishes that you still have. Write them down! How will you honor and celebrate yourself and your life today? Definitely journal about that one.

That IS happiness!

Day 246

Coating everything that is happening with playfulness, well, makes it all playful!

What in your life right now can you coat with playfulness—to shift it from not fun to blissful, from unwanted to wanted, from strict to free? List please!

That IS happiness!

Day 247

Imagine that you are on a mission to make space for your truth!

What or who is standing in your way? List please—then imagine moving what's on your list to the side. Feel the clearing of the direct pathway to your unique YOU!

_____
_____
_____
_____
_____
_____
_____
_____
_____
_____
_____
_____
_____
_____
_____
_____
_____
_____

That IS happiness!

Day 248

I see the best in me. I see the best in you. You see the best in you. You see the best in me.

What "best" will you focus on in yourself? What "best" will you focus on in others?

That IS happiness!

Day 249

Imagine you have a planting tray. Each compartment has a different kind of seed planted inside, every seed has its own space to grow, and none get mixed up; and yet, they are all connected, because of the tray.

How can you leave every single person in your life in their own space—to let them grow, yet still be connected as a whole entity? Is it through unconditional trust and love, or focusing only on your own life?

_____
_____
_____
_____
_____
_____
_____
_____
_____
_____
_____
_____
_____
_____
_____
_____

That IS happiness!

Day 250

Happy mindfulness!

What are you happily mindful about right now? How does this feel? What are you unhappily mindful about right now? How does that feel? How can you shift this unhappily mindfulness to betterment without changing the object—perhaps by shifting your perspective or focus?

That IS happiness!

Day 251

When a loved one has a hard time, you show them compassion and care.

Question is, how can you show that same dedicated compassion, love, and helpfulness to yourself in your new day?

_____

That IS happiness!

Day 252

Love is everywhere, so tune into it!

How will you consciously see, hear, taste, smell, think, and feel all the love that is present in and around you today? I expect nothing less than a stellar list here!

_____
_____
_____
_____
_____
_____
_____
_____
_____
_____
_____
_____
_____
_____
_____
_____
_____
_____
_____
_____
_____

That IS happiness!

Day 253

Imagine that you are looking at all of the clouds in the sky.

Pick your favorite one and make it your emotional home for the day. Enter your cloud! How does it feel in there, peaceful, spacious, like nothingness? How does it it sound, smell, and look in there—calm, beautiful? Spend a lot of time in this cloudy goodness.

That IS happiness!

Day 254

Picture a smiley face that makes you feel happy and joyous!

Stay there for a little! How does the smile make you feel—happy, silly, joyous? How can you focus on smiles and latch onto this wonderful energy today? Creative ideas?

That IS happiness!

Day 255

Imagine that you are planning a magnificent gathering to celebrate life. You choose the location, decoration, food, and drinks. You send out beautiful invitations. All is ready and set to go.

How does that feel? How will you make sure that nothing and nobody can crash your regal gathering of your marvelous new day today?

That IS happiness!

Day 256

"I love..."

What feelings are initiated by this powerful phrase? How often will you say that phrase today? What will you love in your new day? Yourself first—and what or who else?

_____
_____
_____
_____
_____
_____
_____
_____
_____
_____
_____
_____
_____
_____
_____
_____
_____
_____
_____
_____

That IS happiness!

Day 257

Imagine that you are at an outdoor market to buy fresh produce. You pause to take in the beautiful sight of this delicious food. You are very excited, because you get to go and choose the produce that looks the best to you and will make you the happiest.

What best-of-the-best emotions and thoughts will you choose in your new day? What best-of-the-best activities, happenings, and words will you decide to go for? Make your best-of-the-best list!

_____
_____
_____
_____
_____
_____
_____
_____
_____
_____
_____
_____
_____

That IS happiness!

DAY 258

Seriously, don't take everything so seriously!

List what's on your serious list that you will give up and put on your light-hearted list until further notice.

_____
_____
_____
_____
_____
_____
_____
_____
_____
_____
_____
_____
_____
_____
_____
_____
_____
_____
_____
_____
_____
_____

That IS happiness!

Day 259

Imagine a piece of metal in the sun, it is all bright and shiny!

What feelings do you have with "shiny?" Maybe ones like new, luxurious, fun, or "I want it?" What kind of shiny can and will you produce, wear, find, eat, drink, or focus on in your new day?

That IS happiness!

Day 260

Take 3...

When will you take 3 minutes at a time to breathe into your heart today? Be exact and pencil in some "Take 3 time." Hint, hint—once a day is not enough!

That IS happiness!

Day 261

Imagine you are planning a fun party, but only you show up.

Being alone is great, but a little time spent with others can bring unplanned inspirations. How can you spend some time with people to co-create magic—and then return to be a hermit again?

That IS happiness!

Day 262

Think of water and how it moves around rocks. It always finds a way to flow around, above, and even underneath them. Water flows wherever it wants to flow, and does not stop or get held up by the rocks. It keeps its focus on its purpose to flow, and finds other ways around blockages to stay true to itself.

That flow, how does it feel—inspiring, possible, and free? How will you create that type of unstoppable flow for yourself today?

_____
_____
_____
_____
_____
_____
_____
_____
_____
_____
_____
_____
_____
_____
_____
_____

That IS happiness!

Day 263

Imagine that you get to go on a trip to the destination of your choice!

Where will you go? How will you feel, look, and think in that paradise? Be very descriptive here!

That IS happiness!

Day 264

Everything just IS… The good, the bad, the sad, the joyous, the harsh, the angry, and the happy are all the same until you decide how you feel about it.

What in your life right now can you look at with the open attitude of "everything just IS?"

That IS happiness!

Day 265

Imagine a beautiful bird sitting on a branch of a giant tree. After a while, the bird opens his wings to fly to a lower branch of a neighbor tree. He takes off effortlessly, flies free as can be, and lands smoothly on the new branch.

How can you be like that bird—flying freely and with the utmost amount of trust that your next branch is safe? What and whom can you start trusting more? In what will you start believing more, yourself? Your journey?

That IS happiness!

Day 266

It is all about recycling!

What manifestation in your life will you embrace in a fuller and more vivid expansion, then recycle those high-for-life feelings into creating a *higher in energy* future for yourself? How will you focus more on feeling all goodness that is there for you?

That IS happiness!

Day 267

Stop. Sit down. Breathe.

"Today I will breathe myself into_____." Is it health, abundance, happiness? List your needs and set an intention to bless every breath with your demands—to nourish yourself into wholesomeness.

That IS happiness!

Day 268

Surrender!

What will you surrender to in the same way that you surrender yourself into your bed every time? Is it trust, bliss, and enjoyment?

That IS happiness!

Day 269

Stop searching for who you are! First of all, since you are an ever-changing being living in an ever-changing universe, as soon as you find yourself it is old cake because within a second, that is not who you are anymore.

So instead, ask yourself:

- "Who am I right now?"
- "How am I right now?"
- "What am I right now?"

List what comes to your heart and how you will embrace yourself right now!

_____
_____
_____
_____
_____
_____
_____
_____
_____
_____
_____
_____
_____

That IS happiness!

DAY 270

Imagine that you just finished building your house. What a feeling of accomplishment, power, capability, and strength you are shifting to with this happening!

What does a great accomplishment feel like for you? Is it pride, or excitement for being alive? From brushing your teeth to landing a new job, how can you stay focused on these wonderful emotions throughout your new day?

_____
_____
_____
_____
_____
_____
_____
_____
_____
_____
_____
_____
_____
_____
_____
_____
_____

That IS happiness!

Day 271

Think of - and feel - your feet!

How will you pamper your grounding partners - your feet - today? A foot rub, a dance, or by imagining healing light entering your feet? Make your pamper list!

That IS happiness!

Day 272

Love yourself enough to not lose yourself in caring for everything and everyone at all times!

Where can you love yourself more by letting things and others be as is? This shall be your self-love list!

That IS happiness!

Day 273

Co-create magic with the weather! Notice the weather—see, hear, smell, taste, think, and feel its energy.

What incredible energy does the weather have today? Wind—cleansing? Rain—refreshing? Thunder—electric? Snow—pure wonderland? Fog—trusting in solitude? Sun—energizing? Hail—playful and feisty? Clouds—invitation to color-in imagination? How can you latch onto those energies?

That IS happiness!

Day 274

__Imagine you are on a safari expedition. You look to your left and see a lion; then, you look to your right and see a gazelle. Who will you hang out with? Choices, choices!__

How can you use every choice to ask the clarifying question "What is safest, wisest, best, and most fun for me?" What better, happier, or healthier choices will you make today?

That IS happiness!

Day 275

Your lips are very powerful!

How does pulling your lips into a smile feel—happy, healthy, and positive? How can you stay focused on smiling today? Perhaps a smile-now-alarm?

That IS happiness!

Day 276

Imagine a clean, clear, and fresh stream.

How wonderful does that feel for you; pure? Healthy? Clean? How will you ensure that your energy stays this beautifully today? Is it by taking breaks, meditating, slowing down? What fits your day today?

That IS happiness!

Day 277

Words are energy!

What words with an uplifting energy come to your mind? List them and use them in your new day.

That IS happiness!

Day 278

Imagine a breathtakingly beautiful flower tells you all about the parts it does not like on itself, or finds ugly.

What would you say to her? Parallel to that, what would you say to yourself when parts of your whole being are believed to be ugly?

That IS happiness!

Day 279

Feel yourself in love!

How does that feel? What are your thoughts when you are in love? What does the world look like when you are over the moon? Now turn these amazing feelings towards yourself—be in love the same way, with yourself.

That IS happiness!

Day 280

Imagine that you are in a row boat on a river. Down the river is easy to steer and row your boat. Against its flow is really hard and exhausting.

How can you go with the flow—steering yourself down the river of your life in easy-peasy-ness during your new day?

That IS happiness!

Day 281

Don't be afraid to live fully because you are afraid to die!

What fears do you have that keep you from living fully? Put them into this journal, close this book, and consider them locked up in a safe space—for you to go and experience your new day fearlessly.

That IS happiness!

DAY 282

Be flexible!

What flexibility is today's weather asking of you—to be prepared for anything, or to go with the flow? How can you stay flexible with whatever life conditions that come your way?

That IS happiness!

Day 283

A life full of wonders is a wonderful life!

What feelings come up for you with "being in wonder," and what wonders are in your life right now? What wonders can you create for yourself and others today—how can you BE and live more in wonder?

That IS happiness!

Day 284

Imagine that you are sitting down on a comfy sofa. You relax and smile. Your eyes are wide open. You start looking around and acknowledge everything and everyone you see - no matter how you feel about them or it - with saying or thinking "Thank you!"

What do the words "Thank you!" feel like to you? Peaceful, grateful, lovely? What, and who, will you welcome with a "Thank you!" in your new day?

That IS happiness!

Day 285

A great script makes a great movie. A great movie is a great experience and a great experience is happiness.

What is your great script for the best movie ever—your new day? How will you have the most amazing amount of happiness and joy today?

That IS happiness!

Day 286

Imagine that you live on a huge magnificent estate with a humongous mansion. There are plenty of bedrooms, bathrooms, and many entertainment rooms; a dining hall, ballroom, cinema, spa, swimming pool, indoor sports facilities, bowling arena, pool table room, and a casino. And not to forget, the amazing chef's kitchen.

How does this abundance feel? Describe this plentifulness in detail—then copy this "enough of everything" energy into your whole being; your body, mind, soul, and consciousness. Why? Because that is exactly who and what you are—infinitely abundant!

_____
_____
_____
_____
_____
_____
_____
_____
_____
_____
_____
_____
_____
_____

That IS happiness!

Day 287

Pick a feel-good word that touches your heart.

What is your magic word? How does it feel? What creativity and inspirations does it inspire in you? Where can you find your word in your new day? How can you use it often?

That IS happiness!

Day 288

Imagine that you are taking a shower or bubble bath, and a round bit of fluffy foam lands on your nose.

How does this make you feel? Playful, silly, jolly, young? Where can you infuse your life with more play today? Who will you play with? Smile and make your play-list!

That IS happiness!

Day 289

Start a close, loving, and nurturing relationship with your sadness—because your sadness is your true gas meter that your love tank is low or maybe even empty.

How can you fill your love tank today, so your sadness can get a break? By asking your sadness what you need; by following your heart's bliss?

That IS happiness!

Day 290

Imagine that you are walking on the street, and an autumn leaf is blowing behind you.

Do you hear it, do you see it? Will you play with it? Set your written intention to play with what is coming your way today.

That IS happiness!

Day 291

You and water!

A true flow dream-team! Feel the flow in the water of your physical body. How does it feel? How can you create more flow in your life? Is it by being in a state of ease or by becoming one with water through water-play? Make your flow-list!

That IS happiness!

Day 292

Imagine that you admire something in a person.

Today's call to action is to list what you adore in or on others and immediately end the sentence with, "I have that too!" Then, admire that essence in yourself too!

That IS happiness!

Day 293

How much "play" can you find in your new day?

What does "play" mean for you? What emotions does "play" initiate in you? How will you play today? Who will you play with?

That IS happiness!

Day 294

Imagine a beautiful book holding all of your past happenings.

What will you write down in this past-holding book? What right now is on your mind that would, when written down, let you be more in your NOW? Go ahead, leave it all here in this journal, and go newly and freshly into your NOW!

That IS happiness!

Day 295

Start a truthful and honest relationship with your jealousy! Jealousy is personal and different for everyone. You cannot share your jealousy or make others jealous too, like you can share your anger or make others angry too. Your jealousy is your truth and insight into what you want - and need - to do for yourself to fulfill your desires.

Knowing that, be jealous! Then make your jealousy list—or better named, your truth-list!

That IS happiness!

Day 296

Imagine you are in an empty theater choosing the perfect seat.

How can you position yourself to BE and live in the perfect seat today? To get closer to something or someone? Create more distance? Go to the left or right, to move aside? How can you experience your new day in the best view possible?

That IS happiness!

Day 297

Think of a washing machine! It takes little breaks and "slow down" moments while in the cycle of washing the clothes. Sometimes it even stops so the laundry can soak before spinning like crazy again. This guarantees a job well done.

How can you be like a washing machine today—creating slow down moments, or even real stops, in order to do a good job for yourself and in your life?

That IS happiness!

Day 298

Imagine that you got all dressed up, and went to a dance.

How will you let your physical body dance today? How can you make your mind dance freely with your thoughts? How will you allow your soul to dance happily? Let's call this list your "dance moves!"

___
___
___
___
___
___
___
___
___
___
___
___
___
___
___
___
___
___
___
___

That IS happiness!

Day 299

Do you remember when you encountered sparkles as a child?

What feelings do these sparkles bring up for you—playfulness, happiness, lightness, excitement? Where can you notice sparkles in your new day, in raindrops and sunshine? In stores, or getting yourself some glitter? Your sparkle list please!

That IS happiness!

Day 300

Imagine that you are watching the most beautiful sunset ever! It is the sun's way of waving at you, saying "This was a magical day. I am going to shut down now. Let's start new tomorrow. See you bright and early!" Now imagine yourself watching the most beautiful sunrise ever! It is the sun's way of saying "Hello, are you ready to have some fun today? Let's go!"

How will you greet your new day to welcome it sincerely? How will you close your experienced day in the most worthy way—no matter how it went? A gracious morning and night routine is what you are creating here!

_____
_____
_____
_____
_____
_____
_____
_____
_____
_____
_____

That IS happiness!

DAY 301

Being happy is your natural state of being! When you are happy, your physical health is at its peak. Your mind thinks positive thoughts. Your soul feels good and is heard loud and clear. Your consciousness is vivid. Life is going great for you, good things come your way, and nothing (not even the un-fitting) can shift you from being and living in your high-for-life frequency.

How will you ensure your happiness today? What will you do physically, mentally, and soulfully? What happiness will you focus on in your NOW, yourself, and in others?

_____
_____
_____
_____
_____
_____
_____
_____
_____
_____
_____
_____
_____

That IS happiness!

Day 302

Imagine that this is the story of your new day: The first thing you feel is a cold draft in your face coming through the window. Then, while getting ready, you hear a bird chirping in your backyard. When you leave your house, the sun blasts you in your face. On your way to work, you see trees. Later that day the rain gets you wet and on your way home the smell of a bakery fills your nose. Finally back home, you drink a glass of water.

Write about what's in your awareness right now—what's there to feel, hear, enjoy, see, experience, smell, taste, and think of? How will you show gratitude for all the inspiration that is there for you?

_____
_____
_____
_____
_____
_____
_____
_____
_____
_____
_____
_____
_____

That IS happiness!

Day 303

Compliments carry the energy of honor, gratitude, appreciation, kindness, and love.

What is a compliment for you? How does a compliment feel like? Where will you give compliments today and to whom? Yourself, others, happenings? Make your praise-list!

That IS happiness!

Day 304

Imagine that you are in a wildlife park and even though everyone told you about all the wild animals you'd get to see, you see nothing. So, you walk deeper into the park - but still, nothing. You decide to have a seat, and give it some time for the animals to show themselves.

When in your life can you sit down to see what treasures will show once you are still? What situation in your life would greatly profit from such an approach?

That IS happiness!

Day 305

Have an appreciation chat with your physical body!

From head to toe, from limb to limb, from nerve to nerve, from cell to cell; what appreciation will you shower your body with today? When will it be—in the morning while still laying in bed, after a shower when drying yourself, or at night before falling asleep? I say, preferably, as often as possible!

That IS happiness!

Day 306

Imagine waking up and seeing, hearing, tasting, smelling, and thinking only about all magic there is; in you, everybody, and everything.

What does magic feel like for you? What thoughts does magic bring up for you? How do you experience magic and a magical life? How can you create more of that wonderful energy in your new day?

That IS happiness!

Day 307

Stretch your body, mind, soul, and consciousness!

What does stretching feel like for you? Delicious, nice, or initiating an opening-up moment? How will you stretch your physical body today? How will you flex your mind and thoughts? How will you expand your heart and love? How will you spread further into your NOW? Let's see you stretching!

That IS happiness!

Day 308

Imagine that you are at a fork in a road.

Every fork is a choice! How will you become more aware of all the choices in your new day, and how will you nail your choices to perfection—by choosing the one that feels better, is faster, or more convenient?

That IS happiness!

Day 309

Shift yourself, everything, everyone, and the world to happiness!

What is your plan to shift yourself, everyone, and everything to BE and live in a happy frequency today? Maybe sticking "BE happy!" post-it notes everywhere, speaking about joy publicly at the city plaza, or singing loudly about bliss from a tower will accomplish this! What is your plan today?

That IS happiness!

Day 310

Imagine that you are deep cleaning your outside, and inside, while standing under a waterfall.

How does this deep cleaning feel—refreshing, renewing, rejuvenating? How will you stay fresh, clean, and feeling the best ever in your energy? Perhaps through meditation, rest, or movement?

_____
_____
_____
_____
_____
_____
_____
_____
_____
_____
_____
_____
_____
_____
_____
_____
_____

That IS happiness!

Day 311

Being grateful for something is a wonderful frequency to be in. Being "grateful for nothing," however, shifts you to BE and live in an even "higher for life" frequency.

How does gratefulness for something versus being grateful for for nothing feel for you? Does it make you feel unconditionally thankful, happy to just be? When and how will you sit in stillness to practice being grateful for nothing?

That IS happiness!

Day 312

Imagine that you are taking your heart on a love trip!

Where will you go? Around the world, through your country, or the corners of your backyard? What experiences will you have together with your heart—emotions of love, excitement, happiness, joy? Journal about your trip with your heart; the places, your feelings, and the love you will create as a duo. Let your dreams come true and your heart overflow!

That IS happiness!

Day 313

This is a new day! Start fresh, be present, and live simple!

What feelings represent the essence of "new," a "day," and "fresh" for you? What does being present and living simple mean? How can you make your new day as fresh as possible, while focusing on presence and simplicity?

That IS happiness!

Day 314

Imagine you just woke up, and all you can think of, feel, hear, taste, smell, and see is the confidence in you, everyone, and everything.

What does confidence mean for you? What does it feel like? Living through confident eyes, what do you see? How can you show up confidently today? How will you inspire others to be and live confidently too?

That IS happiness!

Day 315

Ask yourself "What energy am I in need of right now?"

Pick your energy, and write how this essence feels—then find something in your life that represents that energy exactly. For example, is it support; the feeling that you are taken care of—could leaning on a wall mean that support for you?

That IS happiness!

Day 316

Imagine that you are looking in the mirror and see a strand of hair in your face. To fix it, you move the strand out of your face. It would never occur to you to touch the mirror and fix your mirror-self.

What are you trying to fix outside of yourself when in reality it demands a shift inside of you?

That IS happiness!

Day 317

What state are you the happiest in?

Is it when you relax, or when you are being a busy bee; when you twirl like a wild one, scream like you never have before, go outdoors or stay a hermit today? Make your happy list!

That IS happiness!

Day 318

Imagine a mountain!

What feelings do you get—strength, tallness, huge or gigantic, being unmovable or unshakable? Write in detail about this mountainous essence. Breathe into it, and BE and live your mountain today!

That IS happiness!

Day 319

Be the Queen or King you are meant to be!

How does that look, feel, sound, taste, and make you think, you being your Queen or King? Journal about your desires to live a regal and grand life—and receiving all this gloriousness.

That IS happiness!

Day 320

Imagine that you are waking up to a fresh new day. All you can see, hear, taste, smell, and think about is the alive-ness and life that is in you, everybody, and everything.

How does that feel? Vivid, powerful, limitless, in wonder and full of energy? How will you drench your new day, yourself, and others in aliveness?

That IS happiness!

Day 321

Close your eyes and visualize water as it shows itself to you.

Feel, hear, taste, smell, see, and think of that water. How do you experience this? As alive, flowing, cool, refreshing, hydrating? How can you be present like that water essence in your new day, and how will you bless all water in you and your life with gratitude?

That IS happiness!

Day 322

Imagine a balcony!

What is your balcony - a space where you can step out, breathe and recharge, or look at something from a different angle - in this new day? Is it a few minutes on an actual balcony, a walk outside, or a moment of silence? How does your balcony look and feel like?

That IS happiness!

Day 323

You, everything, and everyone have a value!

What is your value, physically and energetically? What is the value in the situations and people in your surroundings? Where do you see value of the un-fitting in your life? Make your value list!

_____
_____
_____
_____
_____
_____
_____
_____
_____
_____
_____
_____
_____
_____
_____
_____
_____
_____
_____
_____

That IS happiness!

Day 324

Imagine a street sweeper truck with brushes underneath.

What in your life right now do you want to be swept away, brushed off, or cleansed? How can you use your power to make that happen?

_____
_____
_____
_____
_____
_____
_____
_____
_____
_____
_____
_____
_____
_____
_____
_____
_____
_____
_____
_____

That IS happiness!

Day 325

"Yay! Everything is under control! I am so happy!"
Sounds great, until you lose that control.

What can you accept, respect, appreciate, thank and love by giving up the need to control?

That IS happiness!

Day 326

Imagine a street musician playing the violin to music coming from a stereo.

How does that feel for you? Are you smiling, feeling like you want to dance, or walking with a skip in your step? How will you share your happifying gift with the one-ness of the world, just like that musician?

That IS happiness!

Day 327

Think of your eyes as neutral seers giving you a neutral picture to look at and depending on which glasses you choose to wear, you will see, hear, taste, smell, think, and feel differently about your new day.

What glasses are you going to wear today? The happy, blissful, fun, and joking ones? Or the sad, heavy, and angry ones? Choose your pair and describe how you see your life when looking through them.

That IS happiness!

Day 328

Imagine a fire hydrant. It always has enough water and is ready to give as much as needed. All it requires to unleash is to be connected to the right hose and someone to open the valve, and here it comes flushing and gushing out into the open.

How will you be your energy-hydrant today—always having enough energy, being deeply connected to your soul being, having your gigantic valve wide open, and your essence flushing and gushing through you? Is it by being playful, self-pampering, or by quieting down?

That IS happiness!

Day 329

We all look in the mirror every day, quick and fast to get ready! One last look before we leave. Looking good, let's go! Remember, you are not looking consciously at YOU though. You look in a hurry, without feeling yourself, and most likely while thinking about your new day.

How can you focus on looking consciously at yourself in the mirror—spending quality time with yourself? Possibly by buying a pocket mirror, to have handy at all times?

_____
_____
_____
_____
_____
_____
_____
_____
_____
_____
_____
_____
_____

That IS happiness!

Day 330

Imagine yourself at a cafe getting a cup of coffee or tea, paired with a yummy pastry. You are sending a lot of expectations out there while doing that!

What positive expectations did you set when getting yourself those treats? The anticipation for perfect yumminess, delicious magic, or that the food will be fresh? What phenomenal expectations can you set for your new day?

That IS happiness!

Day 331

Take a heart-break!

How can you shift from hurrying, worrying, stressing, *negative-ing*, and focusing on anything un-fitting to being in your heart—slowing down, trusting, relaxing, *positive-ing*, and giving the fitting in your new day ALL of your energy?

That IS happiness!

Day 332

Imagine that it is nighttime and you forgot where you parked your car. You ask yourself, "Where did I park my car?" retrace your steps, and try to remember where your car is. Next, you turn on the flashlight to bring light into this darkness and situation, and go find your car.

What feels dark in your life right now, physically or energetically? What question can you ask to bring some light into the situation?

That IS happiness!

Day 333

Stay true to yourself. Do all your feel-good doing. But be mindful of how you do it and how everything and everyone around you is impacted by your doing.

How can you BE and live your truth while still being mindful of how you do it, and of how everything and everyone around you is impacted by you doing so?

_____
_____
_____
_____
_____
_____
_____
_____
_____
_____
_____
_____
_____
_____
_____
_____
_____

That IS happiness!

Day 334

Imagine that you are sitting on a beautiful strong horse! You are both excited and ready to go on this riding adventure. At first, you keep the reigns short and tight, which means the horse cannot move or go. You and your horse are stuck. Then, you realize if you loosen the reigns, giving them some playroom, the horse can move and go. Which means you both are off to an amazing ride.

Where in your life are you holding the reigns too tightly? How will you give the universe more room to play with you—to move together and co-create an amazing ride?

That IS happiness!

Day 335

All is going right!

What situation in your life can you infuse with the idea that all is going right, so your expectation shifts to well-expecting and the happening can actually be right?

That IS happiness!

Day 336

Imagine that the first thing you do when you wake up is light a candle.

How does that ceremonial act feel—pampering, regal, special? Now imagine this candle is your inner light and you light it every morning. How does this feel? Gracious, meaningful, enlightening?

That IS happiness!

Day 337

The stage is prepared for you. Everything is ready to start. All this show needs is your powerful YOU to show up and commit to play and live your new day as alive, awake, and vivid as possible. Are you ready?

What does it feel like for you to have your own show? How will you show up as your powerful YOU today? Power-list please!

That IS happiness

Day 338

Imagine that you just rinsed the shampoo out of your hair. Next, you spread the conditioner and find that it is foaming. You grabbed the shampoo bottle again! You laugh (or not) and say, "Stupid me, not paying attention." You rinse, and finally grab the right bottle to condition your hair.

How often do you talk unhealthily about yourself—jokingly or not? What cruel words and phrases about yourself will you not say or think anymore? What will you say instead?

_____
_____
_____
_____
_____
_____
_____
_____
_____
_____
_____
_____
_____
_____
_____
_____

That IS happiness!

Day 339

Being curious automatically opens you up to receive all possible experiences available for you.

What is curiosity for you? How does it feel, think, and look? Is it playful, educational, or even about wanting more? How will you BE and live more curiously today—and what do you expect to happen for you in such a curious frequency?

That IS happiness!

Day 340

Imagine you have that one best friend who always loves you. They bring out the best in you, are always there for you, believe in you, and make you laugh. You feel like this connection is the best thing that has ever happened to you.

Your best friend... It's you that I am talking about! How will you be your best friend? How will you show yourself that you always love yourself? How? Make your "bringing out the best " in me list.

That IS happiness!

Day 341

Co-creation! When you feel good, no matter the why or the what, you are in perfect alignment with who you are, and co-create with the universe.

What do you want to co-create with the universe today? What energy do you need, so that it will be of the highest quality? How can you take yourself and the universe on a happy-spin?

That IS happiness!

Day 342

Imagine that you start your new day by seeing, hearing, tasting, smelling, and thinking only about all of the health there is in you, everyone, and everything.

How does that sound, feel, and look, and what thoughts go with it? Is it energized, happy, abundant, and just so darn good? Make your written promise as a health-focuser!

That IS happiness!

Day 343

Pick a memory when you were the happiest ever!

Journal about it—note your feelings, thoughts, and smiles in that memory. Realize that this "happiest ever" never left! All you have to do is tune back in, again and again.

That IS happiness!

Day 344

Imagine that you are enjoying a brand-new, fresh home cooked meal. Once devoured, you put your dirty plate on the counter until it is time for your next meal. You then take the old crusty plate and put the new fresh food on it. Time to enjoy!

How can you live your new day on a fresh plate so it will taste deliciously and fresh? What will you do to clean out the old—meditation, movement, or throw the old plate out?

That IS happiness!

Day 345

Don't get distracted!

You have the following main focus for your new day: To BE happy! How does that feel? Possibly light? How are you going to keep that focus? What will you do for yourself today to BE happy?

_____
_____
_____
_____
_____
_____
_____
_____
_____
_____
_____
_____
_____
_____
_____
_____
_____
_____

That IS happiness!

Day 346

Imagine a dangling carrot in front of you.

Where in your life are you running after a dangling carrot? Does it feel good, or not? If not, how can you let the carrot come to you, or let the carrot be?

That IS happiness!

Day 347

You are created. You create. Everything is created.

How will you be the amazing creator of your life; through aligning with yourself, minding how you feel, and following your happiness? How will you celebrate all of the creations you have completed, or are in the process of completing—and ones that others have created?

That IS happiness!

Day 348

Imagine you decide to see, hear, taste, smell, and think about all of the abundance there is in you, everyone, and everything.

What is abundance for you—how does it feel, look, sound, taste, and think? How will you allow more abundance into your new day?

That IS happiness!

Day 349

Do it for YOU! Whatever you are doing right now or are about to do, consciously commit to do it for YOU. That insures that all your doings are of a positive nature, enriching you and your experience of life.

How can you shift even the most enduring situation to the essence of the statement "I am doing this for ME?"

_____
_____
_____
_____
_____
_____
_____
_____
_____
_____
_____
_____
_____
_____
_____
_____
_____

That IS happiness!

Day 350

Imagine that you are expecting to watch an action movie, but, the movie has no action in it. First off, it would not count as an action movie. It would not entertain or give you the experience of an action movie. Actually, it would feel boring without the exciting tension. The action makes the movie an action movie.

How can you welcome all conflict in your life, so the fullness of physicality can be experienced and won't get as boring as an action movie without any action?

_____
_____
_____
_____
_____
_____
_____
_____
_____
_____
_____
_____
_____
_____
_____

That IS happiness!

Day 351

Imagine that you are listening to a loved one telling you all about their day.

Set a written intent to listen to your inner voice - your soul being, your energetic part of you - the same way and with the same loving focus that you listen to others.

That IS happiness!

Day 352

Pick your costume!

Who do you need to be today, a fierce pirate? Maybe angelic like an angel; regal like a queen or king, or a playful monkey?

That IS happiness!

Day 353

Have you ever searched for THE magic in your life? You being present in your NOW is THE magic of your life!

What is that magic for you right now? Your breath, a bite of delicious-ness, or a nice sound? How does it feel; magical? How can you keep your focus on all magic today?

_____
_____
_____
_____
_____
_____
_____
_____
_____
_____
_____
_____
_____
_____
_____
_____

That IS happiness!

Day 354

Imagine that you are a beautiful songbird. You are living the life, flying high, eating all the yummy things you can find, and singing the world into a high-for-life frequency. Life is amazing! Until... you see a peregrine falcon waiting for his lunch. What do you do?

Take shelter—what problems or people are you sheltering from? Face it full on—what problems or people are you facing full on? Do these ways feel good, or not?

That IS happiness!

Day 355

Enchantment at its best!

What is enchantment for you? How does it feel, look, sound, think, and taste? Journal about this wonderful energy and about what would enchant you right now.

_____
_____
_____
_____
_____
_____
_____
_____
_____
_____
_____
_____
_____
_____
_____
_____
_____
_____

That IS happiness!

Day 356

When in doubt choose happiness!

What is happiness for you? How does it feel when you are happy? How do you see your life, and yourself, when you are happy? How will you ensure that you choose happiness above all else?

That IS happiness!

Day 357

You are a persistent winner!

No, really! You win because you opened your eyes today, stepped out of bed at some point, maybe even took a shower someday. Giggles aside, find all your wins, feel how they feel, and make your winner-list!

That IS happiness!

Day 358

Pretend that you are an inspector looking for clues and information!

Find proof of what is needed to make yourself feel the best and most amazing about yourself, and ways to make that happen. A thorough inspector-list please!

That IS happiness!

Day 359

Go inward to BE and relax!

Today is all about turning your senses inward—feeling, seeing, hearing, and thinking inward. What does that mean for you? How does that feel for you—like you are aligned? How will you make this wonderful inward-time happen, a bubble bath; mediation, or even walk in nature?

That IS happiness!

Day 360

Imagine a leaf blowing in the wind! There are two energies happening here. There is the leaf being blown around: playful, not in charge, and having a bunch of spontaneous fun. And then there is the wind: absolutely in charge, carrying responsibility, and creating all the power and strength for this happening.

What situations in your life grab your immediate attention? List some. Then ask, "What is better, being the leaf or the wind?" Write your answers, then follow your wisdom.

_____
_____
_____
_____
_____
_____
_____
_____
_____
_____
_____
_____
_____
_____

That IS happiness!

Day 361

Imagine that you have a little glass lantern with a candle inside of your heart. You open the lantern and take the candle into your hands. You see, hear, taste, smell, think, and feel that candle. You come to understand that this is YOUR candle—YOUR light.

How will you light your light today? A smile, a moment of quiet, or a nice hot shower? How will you keep it lit all day long? How does shining your light bright in your new day feel, look, sound, smell, and taste like?

_____
_____
_____
_____
_____
_____
_____
_____
_____
_____
_____
_____
_____
_____
_____

That IS happiness!

Day 362

Be and live like a tree!

How does it feel to be a tree? How will you ground your soul (roots,) strengthen your body (trunk,) and play with your joyful mind (crown?)

That IS happiness!

Day 363

Imagine that you are in front of a candy store!

How does that feel, exciting? What are you going to do—stand outside, step in just a little, or go in all the way? How will you make sure to go into your new day all the way, to grab life by the horns and live sweetly?

That IS happiness!

Day 364

You don't ever need a reason to breathe. You are your breath! It is automatic and always happening for you. It is the same for feeling good.

What reasons to feel good will you kick to the curb—to instead just BE and live feeling good, no matter what?

That IS happiness!

Day 365

Congratulations! You made it! Acknowledge how far you have come in your passion to BE and live in your high-for-life frequency of happiness. See, hear, taste, smell, think, and feel the huge shift you created by showing up every day, reading, journaling, and acting on what you were given to understand, love, and cherish about yourself and your life.

Consciously admire all of the joy that you created for yourself and shared with everything and everyone around you, and be proud of how much better of a world you built for yourself, everything, and everyone.

I applaud you, and hope you celebrate yourself with the highest regard for becoming a happier person. And I trust you'll keep growing in your job as a Happiness Ambassador for All.

Go on, write your heart out about how you will honor yourself, and let the corks pop—making it THE magnificent bash of your happiness!

_____
_____
_____
_____
_____

That IS happiness!

***

And that, my dear reader, is the end of this journal. In truth I could have kept writing for another year making it the longest happiness workbook you have ever done, while probably putting you into an over-saturated state at some point. To avoid that scenario and keep things interesting, I would rather invite you to read one of my other books, listed on the following page, and end the workbook here. And if you haven't already, get yourself the bestseller ***365 Days of Happiness***—the book this journal workbook is the companion to.

I truly hope you enjoyed this workbook as much as I loved creating it. It would be wonderful if you could take a short minute to leave a review on Amazon.com and also on Goodreads.com as soon as you can—your kind feedback helps other readers find my books easier, and get happier faster. Thank you, you mean the whole cupcake to me!

Yours,
    Jacqueline

ALSO BY JACQUELINE PIRTLE

365 Days of Happiness
Because happiness is a piece of cake!

This passage book invites you to create a daily habit to live your every day joy, and is the parent companion to ***365 Days of Happiness***, the journal workbook.

* * *

Life IS Beautiful - Here's to New Beginnings

If you like digging deeper into the meaning of life and are inspired by spirituality, then you'll love Jacqueline's effective teachings.

* * *

Parenting Through the Eyes of Lollipops
A Guide to Conscious Parenting

If you like harmony at home and laughter in the house, then you'll love Jacqueline's inspirational methods.

* * *

What it Means to BE a Woman
And Yes! Women do Poop!

If you like to live free, empowered, and want to decide for yourself, then you'll love Jacqueline's liberating ways.

WANT TO CONTINUE YOUR DAILY HAPPINESS QUEST?

Here is a peak into my book ***Life IS Beautiful***:

BEAUTY AND BEAUTIFUL

Beauty and beautiful is always whatever you want it to be!

The range of what beauty and beautiful means is yours to choose, and can go anywhere from vacationing at the most beautiful place on earth, to wearing the most beautiful outfit ever; or being over the moon about a clean toilet, since it is sheer beauty to sit your bottom onto something that is so squeaky clean.

You are in total charge of your personal relationship to beauty and beautiful!

As we covered in the chapter ***Nothing is Ever Set in Stone***, everything and everyone is energy first and foremost—so are words, feelings, opinions, expectations, and happenings. Everything!

As words, beauty and beautiful carry the energy of special, happiness, bliss, health, nature, betterment, positivity, luxury, glamour, easiness, abundance, wonderful to the eye and heart, a

WANT TO CONTINUE YOUR DAILY HAPPINESS QUEST?

sort of supposed to be like that and naturally as is—and all else that you make it to be.

Seeing, hearing, tasting, smelling, and thinking of - plus feeling - beauty and beautiful is a pure alignment with the untouched natural energetic and physical world, and what it has to offer. This is the natural way of things, until humans strip it away with their actions, ways, and disalignment—then declaring it to be the opposite, ugliness.

Just think of nature and its bountiful wonders. There is nothing but beauty present—even when animals are hunting other animals, the natural beauty of a nourishing value and pure survival is printed in this happening.

This makes for a great case to recondition and align yourself towards beauty all the time, since beauty and beautiful is always there. To think that beauty exists, to hear beauty everywhere, to see the beauty in all, to taste and smell beautifully often, and to feel that beauty is always present in, on, and around you is a powerful clarity—because beauty is inevitable. So why not save your precious energy of the human-proving-it-wrong action to uglify life and instead trust that fact, knowing, and delicious feeling fully and vividly?

Beauty and beautiful is unavoidable and in order to escape it you have to put an enormous effort into dodging and not experiencing it. That effort is exhausting and creates sadness, anger, frustration, and an unlimited amount of unwell-feelings. You might even feel that life is nothing like you want it to be, that none of your desires and wishes are reachable, let alone coming into realization. It's a dilemma that keeps feeding itself by focusing on a reality in which the existence of beauty is denied.

To continue this chapter, buy ***Life IS Beautiful*** to start living fully today!

ABOUT THE AUTHOR

Bestselling author, podcaster, and holistic practitioner, Jacqueline Pirtle, has twenty-four years of experience helping thousands of clients discover their own happiness. Jacqueline is the owner of **FreakyHealer** and has shared her solid teachings through her podcast **The Daily Freak**, sessions, workshops, presentations, and books with clients all over the world. She holds international degrees in holistic health and natural living. Her effective healing work has been featured in print and online magazines, podcasts, radio shows, on TV, and in the documentary *The Overly Emotional Child by Learning Success*, available on amazon prime.

For any questions you might have, to sign up for Jacqueline's newsletter, and for more information or whatever else she is up to, visit www.freakyhealer.com and her social media accounts @freakyhealer.

Made in United States
North Haven, CT
05 March 2023